DATE DUE

APR 0 1 2016			
MAY 1 6 2016			
NOV 2 1 2018			
DEC 1 6 2021			

1st EDITION

Perspectives on Diseases and Disorders

Hepatitis

Jacqueline Langwith
Book Editor

PERSPECTIVES
On Diseases & Disorders

GALE

e • London

Christine Nasso, *Publisher*
Elizabeth Des Chenes, *Managing Editor*

For more information, contact:
Greenhaven Press
27500 Drake Rd.
Farmington Hills, MI 48331-3535
Or you can visit our Internet site at gale.cengage.com

For product information and technology assistance, contact us at

Gale Customer Support, 1-800-877-4253
For permission to use material from this text or product, submit all requests online at www.cengage.com/permissions

Further permissions questions can be e-mailed to permissionrequest@cengage.com

LIBRARY OF CONGRESS CATALOGING-IN-PUBLICATION DATA

Hepatitis / Jacqueline Langwith, book editor.
    p. cm. -- (Perspectives on diseases and disorders)
  Includes bibliographical references and index.
  ISBN 978-0-7377-4553-5 (hardcover)
  1. Hepatitis--Juvenile literature. I. Langwith, Jacqueline.
  RC848.H42H45 2010
  616.3'623--dc22
                                                    2009036458

Printed in the United States of America
1 2 3 4 5 6 7 13 12 11 10 09

CONTENTS

FOREWORD

"Medicine, to produce health, has to examine disease."
—Plutarch

Independent research on a health issue is often the first step to complement discussions with a physician. But locating accurate, well-organized, understandable medical information can be a challenge. A simple Internet search on terms such as "cancer" or "diabetes," for example, returns an intimidating number of results. Sifting through the results can be daunting, particularly when some of the information is inconsistent or even contradictory. The Greenhaven Press series Perspectives on Diseases and Disorders offers a solution to the often overwhelming nature of researching diseases and disorders.

From the clinical to the personal, titles in the Perspectives on Diseases and Disorders series provide students and other researchers with authoritative, accessible information in unique anthologies that include basic information about the disease or disorder, controversial aspects of diagnosis and treatment, and first-person accounts of those impacted by the disease. The result is a well-rounded combination of primary and secondary sources that, together, provide the reader with a better understanding of the disease or disorder.

Each volume in Perspectives on Diseases and Disorders explores a particular disease or disorder in detail. Material for each volume is carefully selected from a wide range of sources, including encyclopedias, journals, newspapers, nonfiction books, speeches, government documents, pamphlets, organization newsletters, and position papers. Articles in the first chapter provide an authoritative, up-to-date overview that covers symptoms, causes and effects, treatments, cures, and medical advances. The second chapter presents a substantial number of opposing viewpoints on controversial treatments and other current debates relating to the volume topic. The third chapter offers a variety of personal perspectives on the disease or disorder. Patients, doctors, caregivers, and loved ones represent just some of the voices found in this narrative chapter.

Each Perspectives on Diseases and Disorders volume also includes:

- An **annotated table of contents** that provides a brief summary of each article in the volume.
- An **introduction** specific to the volume topic.
- Full-color **charts and graphs** to illustrate key points, concepts, and theories.
- Full-color **photos** that show aspects of the disease or disorder and enhance textual material.
- **"Fast Facts"** that highlight pertinent additional statistics and surprising points.
- A **glossary** providing users with definitions of important terms.
- A **chronology** of important dates relating to the disease or disorder.
- An annotated list of **organizations to contact** for students and other readers seeking additional information.
- A **bibliography** of additional books and periodicals for further research.
- A detailed **subject index** that allows readers to quickly find the information they need.

Whether a student researching a disorder, a patient recently diagnosed with a disease, or an individual who simply wants to learn more about a particular disease or disorder, a reader who turns to Perspectives on Diseases and Disorders will find a wealth of information in each volume that offers not only basic information, but also vigorous debate from multiple perspectives.

INTRODUCTION

In the 1980s and early 1990s, receiving news that one was infected with HIV was a literal death sentence. No vaccine or cure for AIDS exists. Back then, people with HIV could expect to become ill with AIDS within about ten years after becoming infected, and then live only one to two years on average after that. The virus destroys immune cells, leaving those infected vulnerable to a whole host of opportunistic infections. Eventually, one of them causes death. Thanks largely to the discovery of a "three-drug cocktail," which became available in 1996, people infected with HIV now live longer and healthier lives. They are not dying anymore from opportunistic diseases with names like toxoplasmosis or Pneumocystis pneumonia. However, a large group of HIV-positive people in the United States struggle with a different kind of opportunistic disease. Many people with HIV are coinfected with hepatitis C. HIV and the hepatitis C virus are similar in a number of ways, and infection with both is a serious problem.

Infection with the hepatitis C virus (HCV) is the most common coinfection in people with HIV. The term "coinfection" refers to being infected with two or more diseases at the same time. Unfortunately for people with HIV, the risk of contracting other infectious diseases is high. Because the two viruses share many characteristics—they are both blood borne RNA viruses that replicate rapidly—HIV-infected people are commonly coinfected with HCV. In the United States, it is estimated that about 15 to 30 percent of all people living with AIDS also have hepatitis C. However, for those who acquired HIV through injection drug use, the prevalence of hepatitis

People who have contracted HIV through injecting drugs are at increased risk of also being infected with hepatitis C. (Publiphoto/Photo Researchers, Inc.)

C coinfection is even higher. It is estimated that from 50 to 90 percent of people who acquired HIV by injecting drugs also carry the hepatitis C virus. In addition to HCV coinfection, people with HIV may also be coinfected with hepatitis B and tuberculosis.

Receiving a diagnosis of hepatitis C is scary, even for people who already have HIV. Gerald Moreno, a past injection drug user with HIV was ecstatic that his HIV was coming under control. It was 1996 and he had just started taking the three-drug cocktail. At a doctor's appointment he learned the good news that his viral load of HIV was coming down. His joy was short-lived, however, when he got news of another infection. Writing about it some ten years later in the Hepatitis C Project's Living with Hepatitis series, Gerald says,

> I remember asking my doctor what this all meant. He answered solemnly that hepatitis C is a very serious disease and could be potentially fatal. I recalled familiar memories of receiving another diagnosis . . . HIV. After a time of self-pity and depression, I called upon the survivor skills that I had learned from HIV: Learn everything that you can because knowledge does equal power. Make the effort to explore the options available to you.

Many HIV-positive people are not aware that they are infected with hepatitis C. The virus rarely causes initial symptoms. Most people find out they have the virus by accident or when it starts causing serious liver damage. In the I-base guide *Hepatitis C for People Living with HIV*, Carmen, a past injection drug user from Spain, recounts how she found out she had hepatitis C:

> I only discovered by accident my hepatitis C status after I volunteered for a trial at my HIV clinic which was looking at whether interferon might be useful for people who had run out of ARV [antiretroviral] options for their HIV. I can't say that it came as a surprise (I assumed it was because of my previous drug use) but never really thought about it as I assumed I would be dead by the time it kicked in.

Before the three-drug cocktail came along, many HIV-positive people felt as Carmen did—why worry about hepatitis C when you have HIV? However, as HIV treatments advanced, Carmen and other coinfected people found that they could no longer ignore their hepatitis

C. As Carmen says, "Now, I am more concerned about the hep C, especially as it is 20 years since I got infected with HIV (I know I picked it up in 1986), and the hep C might have been there even longer."

Carmen is right to worry about hepatitis C, as liver failure from HCV damage is one of the leading causes of death for people infected with HIV. The protease inhibitors and other components of the three-drug cocktail, which is now referred to as "highly active antiretroviral therapy," or HAART, are liver-intensive drugs. As people treat their HIV, the drugs stress their livers and allow the hepatitis C virus to grow more rampant and more deadly. As a result, people who are coinfected with HCV and HIV are more likely than those with HCV alone to develop end-stage liver disease and require lifesaving liver transplants. Unfortunately, many transplant clinics deny organs to HIV-positive people.

The hepatitis C virus (HCV) is shown here in an electron microscope image. Successful HCV treatments can entirely eliminate the virus from a patient's body. (James Cavallini/Photo Researchers, Inc.)

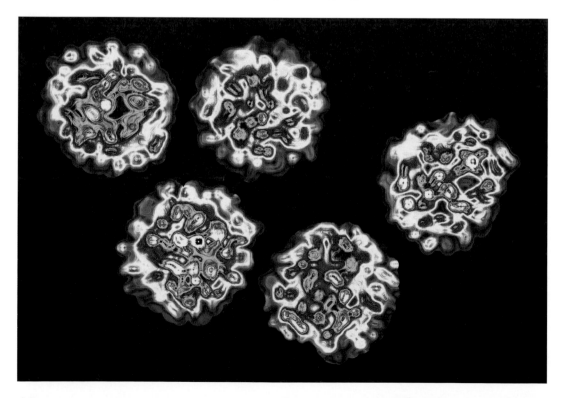

In the past many doctors did not think hepatitis C treatment was wise for HIV-positive patients. Unlike HIV treatment, which only keeps the virus at bay, HCV treatment—if successful—can eradicate the virus from a person's body. However, hepatitis C treatment is physically and mentally grueling, and doctors were leery of its benefits for HIV-infected people. Nevertheless, as the following statement from an HIV physician indicates, doctors are now deciding that hepatitis C treatment can save the lives of coinfected patients:

> While attending the memorial of a coinfected patient who had died from end-stage liver disease, a colleague asked me why I wasn't treating my coinfected patients for hepatitis C. Referring them to a gastroenterologist wasn't working. I was concerned about treating patients with psychiatric comorbidities and/or ongoing substance use. My colleague encouraged me to figure out how, rather than whether, to deliver care to these patients . . . or we would continue to attend funerals of patients dying prematurely from complications of hepatitis C. Since then, my role has changed from gloom and doom—warning patients about side effects—to one of providing education and support and encouraging patients to try HCV treatment.

The hepatitis C virus has created new challenges for many HIV-infected people and the physicians who care for them. In addition to hepatitis C, several other hepatitis viruses are creating new challenges for those infected, for researchers, and for health care providers. In *Perspectives on Diseases and Disorders: Hepatitis*, the authors provide the latest information about the hepatitis viruses, they offer opinions on controversies related to hepatitis, and they provide personal stories about living with hepatitis.

CHAPTER 1

Understanding Hepatitis

An Overview
of Hepatitis

Thelma King Thiel

In the following viewpoint Thelma King Thiel provides an overview of viral hepatitis and its effects on the liver. Thiel outlines hepatitis A, B, and C and their causes. Hepatitis A can be found in human waste and is spread from contact with an infected person or due to unsanitary conditions. Hepatitis B and C are in body fluids and can be transmitted through exposure to sharp instruments contaminated with infected blood or unprotected sex. Although only vaccines against the A and B strains exist, the best protection against hepatitis is to know and avoid activities that aid in its transmission. Thiel is the founder of the Hepatitis Foundation International. She was inspired to raise awareness about liver wellness and hepatitis when she lost her four-year-old son to an incurable liver disease.

P ick up a newspaper anywhere in this country and you are likely to find a story about how viruses are invading and destroying major computer programs that control communication networks, municipal power

Photo on facing page. A young girl is injected with hepatitis A vaccine. There are several types of hepatitis, each requiring a different vaccine. (**Jim Varney/ Photo Researchers, Inc.**)

SOURCE: Thelma King Thiel, "Viral Hepatitis: The Quiet Disease," *USA Today Magazine*, March 1998. Copyright © 1998 Society for the Advancement of Education. Reproduced by permission.

plants, and waste disposal systems. Hepatitis viruses have been causing equally devastating damage to millions of individuals' personal waste disposal system—the liver. This viral-induced shutdown can have an impact on more than 5,000 vital life-preserving functions the liver performs 24 hours a day, silently and efficiently.

Most people are unaware of the important role the liver plays. Some of its tasks include removing toxins from drugs, alcohol, and environmental pollutants; producing clotting factors; metabolizing protein to build muscles, generating bile to aid digestion and help the body absorb nutrients; manufacturing immune factors and hormones; and storing energy. The liver is the body's internal chemical refinery, processing everything we eat, breathe, or absorb through our skin. It is probably the most overworked and misunderstood organ in our body.

The Effect of Hepatitis on the Liver and the Increase in Research Funding

Hepatitis viruses A, B, C, D, and E attack healthy liver cells, causing internal destruction. Sometimes, in hepatitis B, C, and D, the development of scar tissue occurs, called cirrhosis. In essence, the workers in the body's power plant are being destroyed, one by one, until there are not enough left to perform the tasks the liver was created to do. In medical terms, this is known as end-stage liver disease, leading to liver failure and death.

If the liver is such a vital organ, why are most Americans unaware of its importance? Why is so little known about this biological miracle worker? The main reason is that the liver is a non-complaining organ, and thus is its own worst enemy by being a silent workhorse. Often, the first and only sign of a liver disordered is extreme fatigue. All too frequently, that fatigue is blamed on other factors, such as stress or overexertion.

Funding for research to improve the understanding of the physiology and diseases of the liver was abysmally low until the National Commission on Digestive Diseases alerted Congress to the problem in the late 1970s. Since then, funding gradually has increased. However, while Federal funding for AIDS research totals well over $1,000,000,000 annually, $40,000,000 is spent each year to find more effective treatments and cures for viral hepatitis. Nevertheless, with the development of vaccines for hepatitis A and B, improved diagnostic measures to identify several hepatitis viruses, increased success rates for liver transplants, and the advent of patient advocacy groups, liver diseases finally have begun to receive some well-deserved attention.

Misconceptions About Liver Disease and Raising Awareness

My personal interest in liver diseases was motivated by the loss of my four-year-old son, Dean, 27 years ago. Born with a rare and incurable liver disease called *biliary atresia*, he suffered with interminable itching, two fractured hips, jaundice of his skin almost to the point of appearing green, a greatly distended abdomen, and diarrhea everyday. When concerned neighbors learned that he had cirrhosis, they asked me if I drank when I was pregnant. They had no understanding of the importance of the liver and no frame of reference to know how a liver disease could affect the bones in his body. Researchers still do not understand the cause of this childhood liver disease.

Medical experts estimate that 75–80% of liver diseases can be prevented. The most frequently identified are the several forms of viral hepatitis, which strike people from all races, backgrounds, and educational levels, as well as alcohol and drug abusers. The mission of the Hepatitis Foundation International is to heighten awareness of the need for more education and research to prevent the untold human suffering and economic burden caused by liver disease, particularly viral hepatitis.

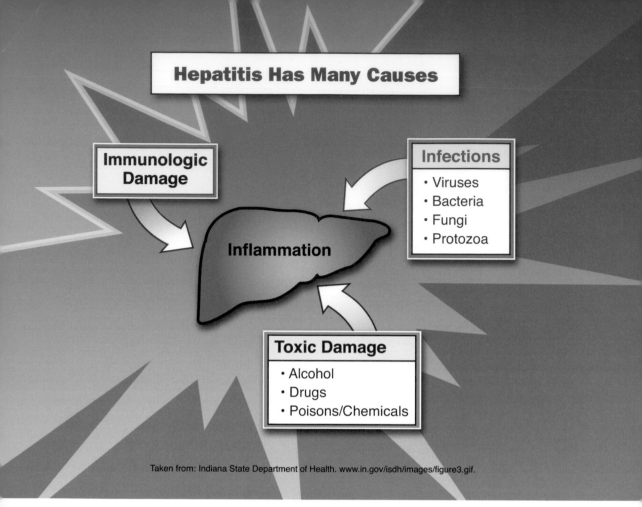

Hepatitis Has Many Causes

Immunologic Damage

Inflammation

Infections
- Viruses
- Bacteria
- Fungi
- Protozoa

Toxic Damage
- Alcohol
- Drugs
- Poisons/Chemicals

Taken from: Indiana State Department of Health. www.in.gov/isdh/images/figure3.gif.

Hepatitis A—the Nuisance Disease

Hepatitis A (HAV) is found in human waste and is spread by close person-to-person contact or by putting anything in one's mouth that has been contaminated by this virus. Eating raw shellfish harvested from contaminated waters or items touched by an infected food handler who did not wash his or her hands after using the bathroom is a common way to contract this illness.

Washing dishes in hot soapy water or a dishwasher usually is sufficient to control the virus. Diaper changing tables, if not cleaned properly or if the covering is not changed after each use, may facilitate the spread of the virus. There is no specific treatment for this disease, but most people recover spontaneously and develop a lifelong immunity to the virus. About one percent of adults who contract HAV develop an overwhelming infection and may need a liver transplant.

Children who have hepatitis A usually have no symptoms, but adults don't fare as well. Many people become quite ill suddenly, experiencing jaundice, fatigue, nausea, vomiting, abdominal pain, dark urine and/or light stool, and fever. Although the incubation period lasts approximately a month, an infected individual can transmit the virus to others as early as two weeks before the symptoms appear and one week after. Symptoms disappear gradually, and complete recovery may take longer. There is no treatment for the disease, which must run its course.

A decade ago, it was estimated that $200,000,000 was lost in work productivity and health care costs each year in the U.S. due to this infection. Today, that figure is estimated to be twice as high. The average person misses about 30 days of work. The good news is that there are safe and effective vaccines to ward off this virus. Hepatitis A vaccine, approved for persons over the age of two, is recommended for gay men, intravenous drug users, anyone who travels to countries with poor sanitary conditions, and children who live in areas that have repeated outbreaks of HAV. For example, Native Americans on reservations and members of closed religious communities, where hepatitis A is common, should consider being vaccinated. Individuals with any form of chronic liver disease should be vaccinated against hepatitis A.

In 1995, there were about 25,000 cases of hepatitis A reported in the U.S. It is thought, however, that the infection rate actually is much higher, with an estimated 125,000 cases. Additionally, Hispanics living in states bordering Mexico have a much higher rate of infection, sometimes exceeding four and five times the national average.

Hepatitis B—the Preventable Epidemic

Found in the blood and body fluids, the hepatitis B virus is 100 times more contagious than HIV and can survive outside the body for at least seven days on a dry surface. Hepatitis B (HBV) can cause inflammation of the liver, which can lead to cirrhosis. In some cases, the disease slowly progresses to liver cancer and even death.

Each year, approximately 100,000 people in this country contract hepatitis B. Of these, 90–95% will recover within six months after proper treatment and develop a lifelong immunity to the virus. However, blood tests always will show that these individuals had been infected with hepatitis B, and blood banks will not accept their blood.

The virus can be passed through unprotected sex and via exposure to sharp instruments contaminated with infected blood, such as needles utilized in tattooing, body piercing, drug use, and acupuncture. The virus can be transmitted through sharing razors, toothbrushes, and nail clippers used by an infected person.

People at risk for contracting hepatitis B also include sexually active gay and bisexual men; those living in the same household with an infected person; anyone with multiple sex partners or having sex with an HBV carrier; people working in occupations that have contact with blood; hemophiliacs; hemodialysis patients; blood transfusion recipients prior to 1975; babies born to infected mothers; prisoners and others in long-term facilities; travelers to developing countries; and adoptees from countries with high rates of HBV.

Effective Vaccines for Hepatitis B

There are safe and effective vaccines available to prevent hepatitis B. In fact, 60,000,000 doses of the vaccine have been administered in this country and there have been no reported serious side effects. Yet, many states have failed to adopt a universal vaccination program. Nationally, it is estimated that this illness costs more than $700,000,000 in work missed and medical costs. In the U.S., there are an estimated 1,000,000 people who have been unable to fight off the virus. Many of these chronically infected individuals are unaware of their infection and unknowingly can spread the disease to others.

The Centers for Disease Control and Prevention recommend that all newborns and 11- and 12-year-olds receive hepatitis B vaccine. By targeting pre-teens, it is possible to control the spread of the virus before children engage in high-risk activities. By vaccinating all newborns, the disease eventually can be eradicated. Many physicians recommend that individuals with any chronic liver disease, including hepatitis C, be vaccinated against hepatitis B to avoid a dual infection that can be devastating to the liver.

> **FAST FACT**
>
> According to the World Hepatitis Alliance, one in twelve people worldwide is living with either chronic hepatitis B or chronic hepatitis C.

Unlike hepatitis A, there is a treatment for this disease—interferon therapy. About half of all chronic HBV-infected individuals are candidates for this therapy, and approximately 35–40% will benefit from treatment. Administered by injection, the treatment may have a number of side effects, including flu-like symptoms, loss of appetite, depression, and fatigue. Regular blood tests are needed during treatment to monitor blood cells, platelets, and liver enzymes. Persons who have hepatitis B should be vaccinated for hepatitis A.

Hepatitis C—the Silent Epidemic

Although discovered in the early to mid 1970s, the hepatitis C virus (HCV), then called non-A non-B hepatitis, could not be identified positively until 1989. Routine screening came quickly thereafter. Spread primarily through close contact with contaminated blood, this complex virus has infected an estimated 3,900,000 Americans, roughly two percent of the population. Similar to hepatitis B, contact

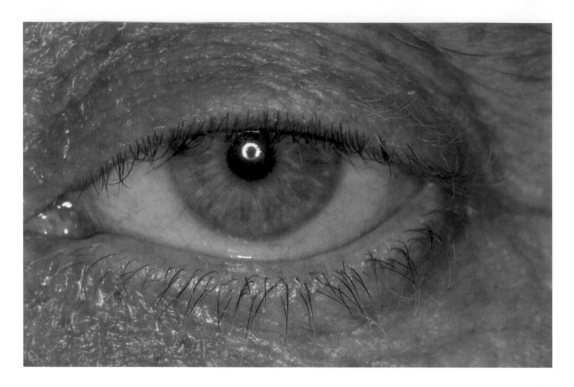

A yellow tint to the whites of the eyes and the skin, called "jaundice," can be a symptom of hepatitis C. (Dr. M.A. Ansary/Photo Researchers, Inc.)

with infected instruments used to puncture the skin can spread the disease. While hepatitis C can be transmitted through sex and from mother to infant during birth, it is not commonly spread in this manner.

A deceptively mild disease at first, hepatitis C generally produces no discernible signs or symptoms. However, the virus is present in the bloodstream and slowly can destroy the liver, causing cirrhosis, liver failure, and even death. Some patients may have symptoms such as fatigue, fever, loss of appetite, and abdominal pain, symptoms that often are confused with the flu. Some also may experience jaundice, a yellowing of the skin and eyes resulting from a malfunction of the liver.

Each year, about 28,000 Americans are infected with the virus. An estimated 50–80% of infected individuals will become carriers of hepatitis C. Medical experts believe this disease progresses slowly over a period of 20 to 40 years. Moreover, HCV currently is the most frequent cause of chronic liver disease in the U.S. About one-third of the nearly 4,000 liver transplant operations performed [annually] in this country are a result of the disease.

There is no vaccine to prevent hepatitis C infection, and efforts to develop one have been stymied by the multiple subgroups of this virus, which frequently coexist in the same patient, and its high rate of mutation. Interferon therapy may suppress the virus after it has entered the bloodstream: about 15% of those treated will have a sustained response.

Long-term therapy, combined with other medications and higher doses of the drug, are yielding better results in suppressing the virus and delaying relapse. Generally, patients under 35 and those who haven't developed cirrhosis have the better response to treatment.

Patients on interferon may experience mild to severe side effects, including fatigue, loss of appetite, fever, abdominal pain, irritability, depression, and anxiety while being treated. Such effects quickly disappear after the treatment is discontinued. Anyone with hepatitis C should not drink alcohol and especially should avoid mixing alcohol with either prescribed or over-the-counter drugs. It is important to tell one's physician what medications are being taken.

Individuals who believe they may have been exposed to either hepatitis B or C should ask their doctor for a specific blood test to determine whether they are infected. Routine blood tests do not screen for either virus. Furthermore, tests may not show positive for several months after exposure to the hepatitis C virus.

Recent preventive measures greatly have reduced the risk of infection, and there are simple steps people can take to protect themselves. Since May, 1990, when screening of blood supplies for the hepatitis C virus began, there has been a sharp drop in the risk of infection from transfusions. In 1981, 10–13% of blood transfusions resulted in HCV infection. By 1992, the risk had dropped to less than one percent. Currently, intravenous drug use with contaminated needles is the chief mode of transmission of hepatitis C.

Snorting cocaine or heroin with an infected instrument may transmit the virus through the sensitive mucous membranes in the nose. In 40% of cases, though, the source of infection is not identified or is unknown. Some experts believe that some infections may result from tattooing, body piercing, and even manicures. Anyone engaging in such activities should inquire about the techniques used to sterilize instruments. If the equipment is disposable or sterilized at high temperatures in a machine called an autoclave, there is little or no danger of transmitting the virus. Since most states do not regulate body piercing or tattoo parlors, individuals who don't inquire about the safety of the instruments being used are playing a game of Russian roulette with their health.

Protection from Hepatitis

While researchers are making some headway in developing treatments, the best protection against hepatitis viruses is to avoid activities that put one at risk of transmission. For those whose occupations call for close contact with blood or blood products or require travel to countries with poor sanitation, vaccinations for hepatitis A and B are recommended strongly. Armed with an understanding of the vital role the liver plays in keeping the body healthy and the damage hepatitis viruses can wreak, readers should take steps to protect themselves and their loved ones against these treacherous viruses.

Hepatitis A Causes a Short-Lived but Potentially Serious Disease

Larry I. Lutwick

In the following article Larry I. Lutwick provides an overview of the disease caused by the hepatitis A virus. According to Lutwick, the hepatitis A virus causes an acute disease that lasts anywhere from two to eight weeks. Unlike hepatitis B and C, hepatitis A does not cause a chronic, or long-term, disease. Lutwick says that hepatitis A is very infectious and is easily spread through contaminated food or water. Children are most susceptible to the disease, but they usually have mild symptoms. Adults who contract hepatitis A generally have more severe symptoms. Lutwick says that a vaccine for hepatitis A became available in 1995. Lutwick is a professor of medicine at the State University of New York and an expert in infectious diseases.

Hepatitis A is an inflammation of the liver caused by a virus, the hepatitis A virus (HAV). It varies in severity, running an acute course, generally starting within two to six weeks after contact with the virus, and lasting no longer than two or three months.

SOURCE: Larry I. Lutwick, "Hepatitis A," *Gale Encyclopedia of Medicine,* 2006. Reproduced by permission of Gale, a part of Cengage Learning.

HAV may occur in single cases after contact with an infected relative or sex partner. Alternately, epidemics may develop when food or drinking water is contaminated by the feces of an infected person.

Risks of Getting Hepatitis A

Hepatitis A was previously known as infectious hepatitis because it spread relatively easily from those infected to close household contacts. Once the infection ends, there is no lasting, chronic phase of illness. However it is not uncommon to have a second episode of symptoms about a month after the first; this is called a relapse, but it is not clear that the virus persists when symptoms recur. Both children and adults may be infected by HAV. Children are the chief victims, but very often have no more than a flu-like illness or no symptoms at all (so-called "sub-

Day care centers are responsible for 14 to 40 percent of all hepatitis A infections in the United States. (© Picture Partners/ Alamy)

clinical" infection), whereas adults are far likelier to have more severe symptoms.

Epidemics of HAV infection can infect dozens and even hundreds (or, on rare occasions, thousands) of persons. In the public's mind, outbreaks of hepatitis A usually are linked with the eating of contaminated food at a restaurant. It is true that food-handlers, who may themselves have no symptoms, can start an alarming, widespread epidemic. Many types of food can be infected by sewage containing HAV, but shellfish, such as clams and oysters, are common culprits.

Apart from contaminated food and water, certain groups are at increased risk of getting infectious hepatitis:

- Children at day care centers make up an estimated 14–40% of all cases of HAV infection in the United States. Changing diapers transmits infection through fecal-oral contact. Toys and other objects may remain contaminated for some time. Often a child without symptoms brings the infection home to siblings and parents.
- Troops living under crowded conditions at military camps or in the field. During World War II there were an estimated five million cases in German soldiers and civilians.
- Anyone living in heavily populated and squalid conditions, such as the very poor and those placed in refugee or prisoner-of-war camps.
- Homosexual men are increasingly at risk of HAV infection from oral-anal sexual contact.
- Travelers visiting an area where hepatitis A is common are at risk of becoming ill.

Causes and Symptoms

The time from exposure to HAV and the onset of symptoms ranges from two to seven weeks and averages about a month. The virus is passed in the feces, especially late during this incubation period, before symptoms first appear. Infected persons are most contagious starting a week or so before symptoms develop, and remain so up until the time jaundice (yellowing of the skin) is noted.

Often the first symptoms to appear are fatigue, aching all over, nausea, and a loss of appetite. Those who like drinking coffee and smoking cigarettes may lose their taste for them. Mild fever is common; it seldom is higher than 101 °F (38.3°C). The liver often enlarges, causing pain or tenderness in the right upper part of the abdomen. Jaundice then develops, typically lasting seven to ten days. Many patients do not visit the doctor until their skin turns yellow. As many as three out of four children have no symptoms of HAV infection, but about 85% of adults will have symptoms. Besides jaundice, the commonest are abdominal pain, loss of appetite, and feeling generally poorly.

FAST FACT

According to the World Hepatitis Alliance, approximately one hundred Americans die each year from hepatitis A.

An occasional patient with hepatitis A will remain jaundiced for a month, two months or even longer, but eventually the jaundice will pass. Very rarely, a patient will develop such severe hepatitis that the liver fails. HAV infection causes about 100 deaths each year in the United States. In developed countries, a pregnant woman who contracts hepatitis A can be expected to do well although a different form of viral hepatitis (hepatitis E) can cause severe infection in pregnant women. In developing countries, however, the infection may prove fatal, probably because nutrition is not adequate.

Diagnosis and Treatment

The early, flu-like symptoms and jaundice, as well as rapid recovery, suggest infectious hepatitis without special tests being done. If there is any question, a specialist in gastrointestinal disorders or infectious diseases can confirm the diagnosis—the detection of a specific antibody, called hepatitis A IgM antibody, that develops when HAV is present in the body. This test always registers positive when a patient has symptoms, and should continue to register positive for four to six months. However, hepatitis A IgM antibody will persist lifelong in the blood and is protective against reinfection.

Once symptoms appear, no antibiotics or other medicines will shorten the course of infectious hepatitis. Patients should rest in bed as needed, take a healthy diet, and avoid drinking alcohol and/or any medications that could further damage the liver. If a patient feels well it is all right to return to school or work even if some jaundice remains.

Prognosis and Prevention

Most patients with acute hepatitis, even when severe, begin feeling better in two to three weeks, and recover completely in four to eight weeks. After recovering from hepatitis A, a person no longer carries the virus and remains immune for life. In the United States, serious complications are infrequent and deaths are very rare. In the United States, as many as 75% of adults over 50 years of age will have blood test evidence of previous hepatitis A.

The single best way to keep from spreading hepatitis A infection is to wash the hands carefully after using the toilet. Those who are infected should not share items that might carry infection. Special care should be taken to avoid transmitting infection to a sex partner. Travelers should avoid water and ice if unsure of their purity, or they can boil water for one minute before drinking it. All foods eaten should be packaged, well cooked or, in the case of fresh fruit, peeled.

If exposure is a possibility, infection may be prevented by an injection of a serum fraction containing antibody against HAV. This material, called immune serum globulin (ISG), is 90% protective even when injected after exposure—providing it is given within two weeks. Anyone living with an infected patient should receive ISG. For long-term protection, a killed virus hepatitis A vaccine became available in 1995. More than 95% of those vaccinated will

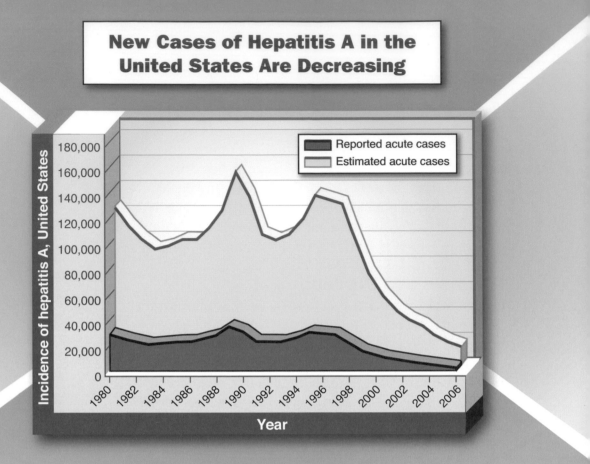

New Cases of Hepatitis A in the United States Are Decreasing

Incidence of hepatitis A, United States

Reported acute cases
Estimated acute cases

Year

Taken from: Centers For Disease Control and Prevention, www.cdc.gov/hepatitis/PDFs/disease_burden.pdf.

develop an adequate amount of anti-HAV antibody. Those who should consider being vaccinated include healthcare professionals, those working at day care and similar facilities, frequent travelers to areas with poor sanitation, those with any form of chronic liver disease, and those who are very sexually active. Starting in 2000, routine immunization with the hepatitis A vaccine was recommended for children born in states where the rate of hepatitis A was two or more times the national average (Alaska, Arizona, California, Idaho, Nevada, New Mexico, Oklahoma, Oregon, South Dakota, Utah, and Washington) and suggested in states where the rate was 1.5 times the national average (Arkansas, Colorado, Missouri, Montana, Texas and Wyoming).

Hepatitis B Is One of the Most Common Chronic Infectious Diseases

David A. Cramer and Teresa G. Odle

In the following selection David A. Cramer and Teresa G. Odle provide an overview of the disease caused by the hepatitis B virus. According to the authors, many people are unaware that they carry—and can spread—the hepatitis B virus. The virus causes two different forms of the disease, an acute form and a chronic form. Acute hepatitis B, which is common in younger adults, generally lasts for about two to three months and causes nausea, loss of appetite, and a feeling of pain or tenderness in the right side of the upper abdomen. Hepatitis B diseases lasting longer than six months are called chronic. Typically, over time, chronic hepatitis B causes liver scarring, which can lead to liver cancer. According to the authors, there is a safe and effective vaccine that can prevent hepatitis B infection. Cramer and Odle are nationally recognized medical writers.

Hepatitis B is a potentially serious form of liver inflammation due to infection by the hepatitis B virus (HBV). It occurs in both rapidly developing

SOURCE: David A. Cramer and Teresa G. Odle, "Hepatitis B," *Gale Encyclopedia of Medicine*, 2006. Reproduced by permission of Gale, a part of Cengage Learning.

(acute) and long-lasting (chronic) forms, and is one of the most common chronic infectious diseases worldwide. An effective vaccine is available that will prevent the disease in those who are later exposed.

Many People Worldwide Carry the Virus

Commonly called "serum hepatitis," hepatitis B ranges from mild to severe. Some people who are infected by HBV develop no symptoms and are totally unaware of the fact, but they may carry HBV in their blood and pass the infection on to others. In its chronic form, HBV infection may destroy the liver through a scarring process, called cirrhosis, or it may lead to cancer of the liver.

When a person is infected by HBV, the virus enters the bloodstream and body fluids, and is able to pass through tiny breaks in the skin, mouth, or the male or female genital area. There are several ways of getting the infection:

- During birth, a mother with hepatitis B may pass HBV on to her infant.
- Contact with infected blood is a common means of transmitting hepatitis B. One way this may happen is by being stuck with a needle. Both health care workers and those who inject drugs into their veins are at risk in this way.
- Having sex with a person infected by HBV is an important risk factor (especially anal sex).

Although there are many ways of passing on HBV, the virus actually is not very easily transmitted. There is no need to worry that casual contact, such as shaking hands, will expose one to hepatitis B. There is no reason not to share a workplace or even a restroom with an infected person.

More than 300 million persons throughout the world are infected by HBV. While most who become chronic carriers of the virus live in Asia and Africa, there are

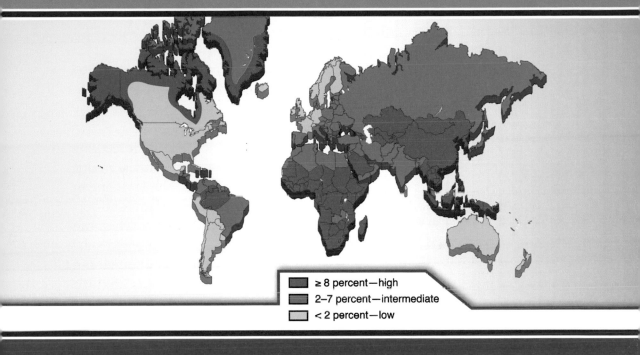

Worldwide Prevalence of Chronic Hepatitis B

≥ 8 percent—high
2–7 percent—intermediate
< 2 percent—low

Taken from: D. Lavanchy, World Health Organization, Communicable Diseases Surveillance and Response.

no fewer than 1.5 million carriers in the United States. Because carriers represent a constant threat of transmitting the infection, the risk of hepatitis B is always highest where there are many carriers. Such areas are said to be endemic for hepatitis B. When infants or young children living in an endemic area are infected, their chance of becoming a chronic hepatitis B carrier is at least 90%. This probably is because their bodies are not able to make the substances (antibodies) that destroy the virus. In contrast, no more than 5% of infected teenagers and adults develop chronic infection.

With the exception of HBV, all the common viruses that cause hepatitis are known as RNA viruses because they contain ribonucleic acid or RNA as their genetic material. HBV is the only deoxyribonucleic acid or DNA virus that is a major cause of hepatitis. HBV is made up of several fragments, called antigens, that stimulate the body's immune system to produce the antibodies that can neutralize or even destroy the infecting virus. It is, in fact, the immune reaction, not the virus, that seems to cause the liver inflammation.

Acute Hepatitis B

In the United States, a majority of acute HBV infections occur in teenagers and young adults. Half of these youth never develop symptoms, and only about 20%—or one in five infected patients—develop severe symptoms and yellowing of the skin (jaundice). Jaundice occurs when the infected liver is unable to get rid of certain colored substances, or pigments, as it normally does. The remaining 30% of patients have only "flu-like" symptoms and will probably not even be diagnosed as having hepatitis unless certain tests are done.

The most common symptoms of acute hepatitis B are loss of appetite, nausea, generally feeling poorly, and pain or tenderness in the right upper part of the abdomen (where the liver is located). Compared to patients with hepatitis A or C, those with HBV infection are less able to continue their usual activities and require more time resting in bed.

Occasionally patients with HBV infection will develop joint swelling and pain (arthritis) as well as hives or a skin rash before jaundice appears. The joint symptoms usually last no longer than three to seven days.

Typically the symptoms of acute hepatitis B do not persist longer than two or three months. If they continue for four months, the patient has an abnormally long-lasting acute infection. In a small number of patients—probably fewer than 3%—the infection keeps getting worse as the liver cells die off. Jaundice deepens, and patients may bleed easily when the levels of coagulation factors (normally made by the liver) decrease. Large amounts of fluid collect in the abdomen and beneath the skin (edema). The least common outcome of acute HBV infection, seen in fewer than 1% of patients, is fulminant hepatitis, when the liver fails entirely. Only about half of these patients can be expected to live.

Chronic Hepatitis B

HBV infection lasting longer than six months is said to be chronic. After this time it is much less likely for the infection to disappear. Not all carriers of the virus develop chronic liver disease; in fact, a majority have no symptoms. But, about one in every four HBV carriers develop liver disease that gets worse over time, as the liver becomes more and more scarred and less able to carry out its normal functions. A badly scarred liver is called cirrhosis. Patients are likely to have an enlarged liver and

A human liver shows the effects of chronic hepatitis B. About 25 percent of HBV carriers will develop liver disease. (Martin M. Rotker/Photo Researchers, Inc.)

spleen, as well as tiny clusters of abnormal blood vessels in the skin that resemble spiders. . . .

The most serious complication of chronic HBV infection is liver cancer. Worldwide this is the most common cancer to occur in men. Nevertheless, the overall chance that liver cancer will develop at any time in a patient's life is probably much lower than 10%. Patients with chronic hepatitis B who drink or smoke are more likely to develop liver cancer. It is not unusual for a person to simultaneously have both HBV infection and infection by HIV (human immunodeficiency virus, the cause of AIDS). A study released in 2003 reported that men infected with both HIV and HBV were more likely to die from liver disease than people infected with just one of the diseases.

Diagnosis, Treatment, and Prognosis

Hepatitis B is diagnosed by detecting one of the viral antigens—called hepatitis B surface antigen (HBsAg)—in the blood. Later in the acute disease, HBsAg may no longer be present, in which case a test for antibodies to a different antigen—hepatitis B core antigen—is used. If HBsAg can be detected in the blood for longer than six months, chronic hepatitis B is diagnosed. A number of tests can be done to learn how well, or poorly, the liver is working. They include blood clotting tests and tests for enzymes that are found in abnormally high amounts when any form of hepatitis is present.

In the past, there was no treatment available for hepatitis B. But developments have been made in recent years on drugs that suppress the virus and its symptoms. In early 2003, a drug called adefovir was reported as an effective treatment. Another drug called tenofovir was demonstrated as effective in patients infected with both hepatitis B and HIV. Two studies also reported on the effectiveness of a drug called Preveon, which was more expensive than others. Patients also should rest in bed as needed, continue to eat a healthy diet, and avoid alcohol. Any non-critical surgery should be postponed.

Each year an estimated 150,000 persons in the United States get hepatitis B. More than 10,000 will require hospital care, and as many as 5,000 will die from complications of the infection. About 90% of all those infected will have acute disease only. A large majority of these patients will recover within three months. It is the remaining 10%, with chronic infection, who account for most serious complications and deaths from HBV infection. In the United States, perhaps only 2% of all those who are infected will become chronically ill. The course of chronic HBV infection in any particular patient is unpredictable. Some patients who do well at first may later develop serious complications. Even when no symptoms of liver disease develop, chronic carriers remain a threat to others by serving as a source of infection.

> **FAST FACT**
>
> According to the World Health Organization, about 2 billion people worldwide have been infected with the hepatitis B virus.

Prevention

The best way to prevent any form of viral hepatitis is to avoid contact with blood and other body fluids of infected individuals. The use of condoms during sex also is advisable.

If a person is exposed to hepatitis B, a serum preparation containing a high level of antibody against HBV may prevent infection if given within three to seven days of exposure. Babies born of a mother with HBV should receive the vaccine within 24 hours. An effective and safe vaccine is available that reliably prevents hepatitis B. Vaccination is suggested for most infants and for children aged 10 and younger whose parents are from a place where hepatitis B is common. Teenagers not vaccinated as children and all adults at risk of exposure also should be vaccinated against hepatitis B. Three doses are recommended.

Those at increased risk of getting hepatitis B, and who therefore should be vaccinated, include:

- household contacts of a person carrying HBV
- healthcare workers who often come in contact with patients' blood or other body fluids
- patients with kidney disease who periodically undergo hemodialysis [removal of waste products from the blood]
- homosexual men who are sexually active, and heterosexuals who have multiple sex partners
- persons coming from areas where HBV infection is a major problem
- prisoners and others living in crowded institutions
- drug abusers who use needles to inject drugs into their veins

Studies released in 2003 showed increased risk of non-response to hepatitis B vaccines among adults over age 30. This may be related to age-associated changes in the immune system.

Hepatitis C Can Go Undetected for Years

Larry I. Lutwick and Tish Davidson

In the following selection Larry I. Lutwick and Tish Davidson provide an overview of the disease caused by the hepatitis C virus. According to Lutwick and Davidson, hepatitis C is a serious and chronic disease that affects 170 million or more people worldwide. Many people are unaware that they have the virus, as its initial symptoms are usually quite mild. However, over time hepatitis C can progress and cause severe liver damage leading to liver cancer, cirrhosis of the liver, and eventually liver failure. According to the authors, a vaccine has not yet been developed for the hepatitis C virus. Lutwick is a professor of medicine at the State University of New York and an expert on infectious diseases. Davidson is a nationally published health and medical writer.

Hepatitis C is one of six (as of 2007) identified hepatitis viruses. The Hepatitis C virus (HCV) was suspected as early as 1974 but was not identified until 1989. It is a blood-borne virus that was the

SOURCE: Larry I. Lutwick and Tish Davidson, "Hepatitis C," *Gale Encyclopedia of Medicine,* 2007. Reproduced by permission of Gale, a part of Cengage Learning.

major cause of "transfusion hepatitis," which can develop in patients who are given blood or most blood products in the United States before 1992. Thereafter, tests were devised to detect the virus in blood units before transfusing them. As a result, since the early 1990s transfused blood is less commonly the cause of hepatitis C.

The hepatitis C form of hepatitis is generally mild in its early, acute stage, but it is much more likely than hepatitis B (85% as compared to 10%) to progress to chronic liver disease. In addition, more than two of every three persons who are infected by HCV may continue to have the virus in their blood and so become carriers who can transmit the infection to others.

Risks, Causes, and Symptoms

Before the 1990s, many people became infected with HCV through blood transfusions. In 2007, the most common ways of transmitting HCV are through sharing needles (almost 60% of infections), accidentally being exposed to contaminated blood (about 10% of cases), or receiving a tattoo done with a contaminated needle. Less frequent methods of transmission are from infected mother to child during childbirth, and a rare method is from sexual intercourse with an infected person. Transmission may take place with either heterosexual or homosexual behavior.

Those at increased risk of developing hepatitis C include:

- healthcare workers who come in contact with infected blood from a cut or bruise, or from a device or instrument that has been infected ("contaminated")
- persons who inject illicit drugs into their veins and skin, especially if they share needles and syringes with other users
- anyone who gets a tattoo or has his or her skin pierced with an infected needle
- persons who received blood transfusions before 1992
- persons who are receiving kidney dialysis

Many people who are infected with HCV do not have any of these risk factors. Nevertheless, the World Health Organization estimated that in 2006, 170 million people worldwide were infected with HCV. In the United States, the Centers for Disease Control and Prevention (CDC) estimated that 1.8% of the population carried the virus. In 2006, about 30,000 new cases of hepatitis C were diagnosed in the United States and the virus caused between 8,000 and 10,000 deaths. In the United States, 65% of infected individuals are between the ages of 30 and 49. African Americans and Hispanics have a higher rate of infection than whites. People who acquire the infection at a younger age tend to have better outcomes than those who are infected when they are older, and women tend to have better outcomes than men.

> **FAST FACT**
>
> According to the Hepatitis Foundation International, 3 percent of the world's population is infected with HCV.

Acute (newly developed) hepatitis C is rarely observed, as the early disease is generally quite mild. More than half of all individuals who develop hepatitis C have no symptoms or signs. Some, however, may have a minor illness with flu-like symptoms. Any form of hepatitis may keep the liver from eliminating certain colored (pigmented) substances as it normally does. These pigments collect in the skin, turning it yellow, along with the whites of the eyes. About one in four patients with hepatitis C will develop this yellowing of the skin called jaundice. Some people lose their appetite and frequently feel tired or may feel nauseous or vomit.

In most patients, HCV can still be found in the blood six months after the start of acute infection, and these patients are considered to be carriers. If the virus persists for one year, it is unlikely to disappear. About 20% of chronic carriers develop cirrhosis (scarring) of the liver when the virus damages or destroys large numbers of liver cells, which are then replaced by scar tissue. Cirrhosis may develop only after a long period (as long as 20–30 years). Most (four in five) patients will not develop cirrhosis and instead have a mild, chronic form of infection called chronic persistent hepatitis and when they die, will die with, not of, the infection.

Nevertheless, patients with chronic HCV infection are at risk of developing certain very serious complications. About one-third of people with chronic HCV infection who develop cirrhosis suffer liver failure within 10 years. Between 1% and 4% of people with chronic HCV infection go on to develop hepatocellular carcinoma (HCC), a type of liver cancer.

Diagnosis and Treatment

Hepatitis C should be suspected if a patient develops jaundice and reports recent contact with the blood of a person who may have been infected. A blood test is available to detect the HCV antibody, a substance that the body makes to combat HCV. The test is about 97% accurate, but does not distinguish between acute and chronic infection. It indicates whether a person has ever been infected, but cannot distinguish whether the virus is still present. Several other blood tests are available to test for HCV RNA (the genetic material of the virus). These tests can be performed in early infection before the antibody is measurable. Simpler blood tests can be done to show how much jaundice-causing pigment is in a patient's blood, or to measure the levels of certain enzymes (proteins) made by the liver. High levels of these liver enzymes (called ALT and AST) indicate that the liver is inflamed. Rising levels could suggest that the infection is getting worse. A liver biopsy (removing a small amount of tissue with a thin needle) can also be used to diagnose hepatitis C.

The goal of treatment is to rid the body of the hepatitis C virus. The National Institutes of Health recommend that anyone who has a positive test for the HCV virus in their blood, a liver biopsy that indicates liver damage, or an elevated amount of the liver enzyme ALT receive

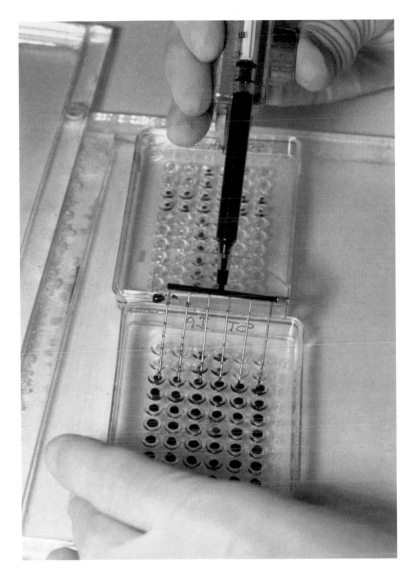

The ELISA blood test (pictured) measures the levels of certain enzymes in a patient's liver. Abnormal levels indicate that the hepatitis C virus is present. (**Klaus Guldbrandsen/Photo Researchers, Inc.**)

treatment. Some controversy exists on how elevated the ALT level should be before treatment is begun.

Drug therapy involves treatment with pegylated interferon alfa combined with twice-daily oral doses of ribavirin (Rebetol), an antiviral agent. As of 2007, three different genotypes (variants) of the hepatitis C virus had been identified. Individuals with genotype 1, the most common genotype in the United States, are usually given

48 weeks of drug treatment, while those with genotypes 2 and 3 are given a 24-week treatment. If this regimen does not eradicate the virus, it may be repeated once. These drugs may have unpleasant flu-like side effects and may cause extreme fatigue, skin irritation, anemia (too few red blood cells) problems with memory and concentration, depression and suicidal behavior, especially in people who have a history of depression.

When hepatitis destroys most or all of the liver, the only hope may be a liver transplant. However, suitable donor livers are often difficult to find. Liver transplantation does not cure hepatitis C. The new liver usually becomes infected by HCV and may go on to develop cirrhosis or cancer.

Prognosis and Prevention

In roughly one-fifth of patients who develop hepatitis C, the acute infection will subside, and they will recover completely within four to eight weeks without treatment and have no later problems. Other patients face two risks: they may develop chronic liver infection and possibly serious complications such as cirrhosis and liver cancer, and they will continue carrying the virus and may pass it on to others. Drug therapy cures about 50% of people infected with the type 1 genotype of HCV and about 80% of those infected with type 2 or 3 genotype.

No vaccine has yet been developed to prevent hepatitis C in persons exposed to the virus. There are, however, many ways in which infection may be avoided:

- Those who inject drugs should never share needles, syringes, swabs, spoons, or anything else that is exposed to bodily fluids. They should always use clean equipment.
- Hands should be washed before and after contact with another person's blood or if the skin is penetrated.

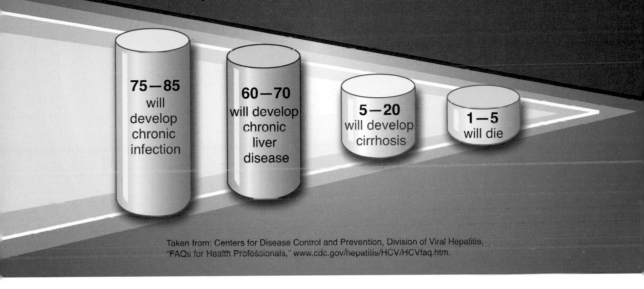

HCV Infections: Prognoses

Of every one hundred persons infected with HCV:

75—85 will develop chronic infection

60—70 will develop chronic liver disease

5—20 will develop cirrhosis

1—5 will die

Taken from: Centers for Disease Control and Prevention, Division of Viral Hepatitis, "FAQs for Health Professionals," www.cdc.gov/hepatitis/HCV/HCVfaq.htm.

- The sharing of personal items should be avoided, particularly those that can puncture the skin or inside of the mouth, such as razors, nail files and scissors, and even toothbrushes.
- Condoms should be used for either vaginal or oral sex.

If a person does develop hepatitis C, its spread may be prevented by:

- not donating blood
- not sharing personal items with others
- wiping up any spilled blood while using gloves, household bleach, and disposable paper towels
- carefully covering any cut or wound with a Band-Aid or dressing
- practicing safe sex, especially during the acute phase of the infection

Hepatitis D Has Little Public Awareness

Hepatitis B Foundation

In the following article the Hepatitis B Foundation, in its newsletter *B Informed*, discusses a little-known hepatitis virus, hepatitis D. According to researchers, hepatitis D is one of the most severe forms of viral hepatitis. However, hepatitis D can never act alone. It is a parasite and depends on another of the hepatitis viruses, hepatitis B, to make part of its viral machinery. Functioning together, hepatitis B and D can cause an extremely severe and fast-acting liver disease, say the *B Informed* authors. The Hepatitis B Foundation is an American nonprofit organization dedicated to the global problem of hepatitis B.

Hepatitis D virus (HDV)—the "D" is for delta—is a viral enigma [mystery] that doesn't act like a normal virus. It is helpless—that is, it can't infect a cell—without its viral accomplice, the hepatitis B virus (HBV), and makes infection with HBV worse.

Delta virus can only cause illness in those already infected with HBV, said Timothy Block, Ph.D., director

SOURCE: "Hepatitis D Flies Under the Radar Screen," *B Informed*, July 6, 2006. Copyright © 2006 Baldwin Publishing. Reproduced by permission.

and professor of the Drexel University Institute for Biotechnology and Virology Research.

One of the Most Severe Forms of Viral Hepatitis

"It can take quiescent [inactive] HBV and turn it into an acute, lethal viral infection," Block said. "Liver disease—cirrhosis, liver failure—that might take decades to develop or could only take a year or two. Delta virus converts HBV infection into an emergency situation."

"It's one at the most severe forms of human viral hepatitis," said Jeffrey Glenn, M.D., Ph.D., assistant professor of medicine at Stanford University School

When a patient is infected with both the hepatitis B and hepatitis D viruses, the effects on the liver are devastating, as shown here.
(Martin M. Rotker/Photo Researchers, Inc.)

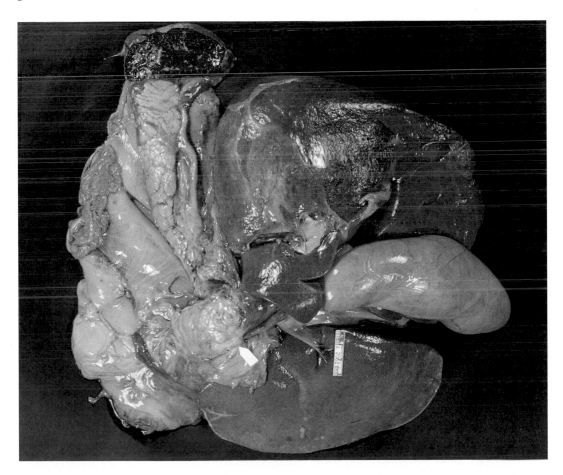

of Medicine. "Delta virus is a parasite of HBV because it encodes its own genome and coat-like protein but it doesn't make its own envelope protein," Glenn explained. "It steals that from HBV. It needs the B envelope protein to make its own, and this provides a means to infect new cells and subsequently make a fully formed viral particle to get out of those cells to infect others."

Individuals can acquire delta virus two ways: Either after infection with HBV, which is called a "superinfection" and more likely to stay chronic, or a "co-infection," which entails becoming infected with both viruses at the same time. In the latter, acute infections are more severe and increase the likelihood of developing liver disease much more quickly.

Perhaps 10 to 15 million worldwide are infected, though fewer than 100,000 in the U.S. have the virus. It is concentrated in particular regions worldwide. Mediterranean areas—southern Italy and southern Greece, for example—have larger than usual numbers of affected individuals, and in Turkey it is endemic.

Some believe its incidence is declining. "As a disease it's disappearing, probably a result of the HBV vaccine and a reduced number of HBV carriers," said John Taylor, Ph.D., senior member at Fox Chase Cancer Center.

> **FAST FACT**
>
> According to the U.S. National Institutes of Health, hepatitis D infects about 15 million people worldwide.

Flies Under the Radar

Because HDV is not a huge problem in the U.S., it flies under the radar screen of public awareness. Screening for HDV is not routinely ordered; however, infection with delta virus should always be considered when a patient with chronic liver disease suddenly gets worse, said Taylor.

Researchers have been frustrated in their attempts to develop effective treatments against HDV. Newer antiviral drugs that keep down levels of HBV DNA don't do much against delta virus because they don't affect the

HBV envelope protein. The antiviral drug lamivudine, for example, reduces HBV DNA yet doesn't touch its envelope protein. And interferon hasn't helped much thus far.

With research there is always hope. Glenn and his co-workers have discovered that the delta antigen is modified by a specific lipid called a prenylipid in a process known as prenylation, which is necessary to make a delta virus particle. "Preventing this means no particles are made," he said. "A drug that could prevent prenylation of delta antigen could be a practical therapy."

His research team is looking at the effectiveness of potential drugs in progressively advanced models of delta

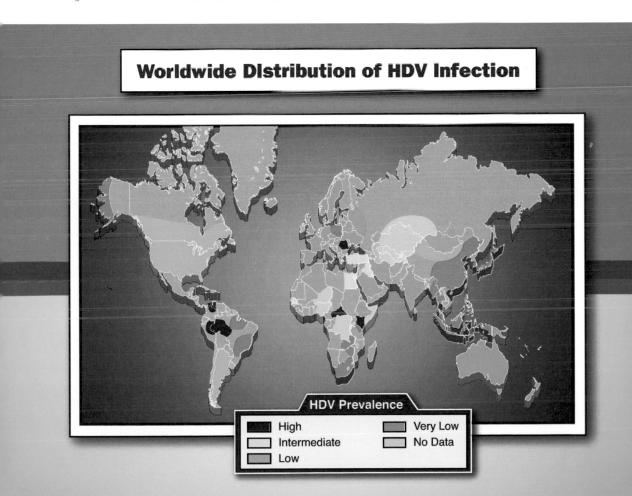

Worldwide Distribution of HDV Infection

HDV Prevalence

- High
- Intermediate
- Low
- Very Low
- No Data

Taken from: Centers for Disease Control and Prevention.

infection. More recently, they established a mouse model of delta virus infection and completely cleared the virus from the blood of mice using these drugs.

Promising Research

"We've been working on these for the last decade and think they hold much promise," Glenn said. "We're hoping sometime in the next year to do the first human trial of a drug specifically targeting this process."

Fox Chase's Taylor said that understanding how delta virus infects new cells could provide keys to how HBV enters new cells. "The delta studies have come a long way, but we need to understand more about its behavior before we can find effective drugs."

A New Hepatitis B Vaccine May Help Those in the Developing World

ScienceDaily

In the following article *ScienceDaily* reports on a hepatitis B vaccine breakthrough from the Michigan Nanotechnology Institute for Medicine and Biological Sciences at the University of Michigan. According to *ScienceDaily*, researchers from the institute have created a hepatitis B vaccine, which is delivered via a superfine emulsion of soybean oil, water, and alcohol. Instead of receiving a needle injection containing the vaccine, people inhale the vaccine emulsion. The vaccine is an example of nanotechnology-based medicine; each droplet in the vaccine emulsion is less than 400 nanometers in size (a single nanometer is one billionth of a meter). According to *ScienceDaily*, the new vaccine should help people in third world countries because it generally does not need refrigeration, it only requires two administrations rather than three, and it avoids the risk of spreading needle-borne diseases. *ScienceDaily* is an online news source that showcases science news stories from the world's leading universities and research organizations.

SOURCE: "Nano Vaccine for Hepatitis B Produces Strong Immunity," University of Michigan Health System News Release, August 13, 2008. Reproduced by permission.

Chronic hepatitis B infects 400 million people worldwide, many of them children. Even with three effective vaccines available, hepatitis B remains a stubborn, unrelenting health problem, especially in Africa and other developing areas. The disease and its complications cause an estimated 1 million deaths globally each year.

Vaccination Faces Obstacles in Poor Countries

In many poor countries, refrigerated conditions required for the current vaccines are costly and hard to come by. It's often difficult in the field to keep needles and syringes sterile. The need to have people return for the three shots currently required also limits success.

Now, a new vaccine that avoids these drawbacks has moved a step closer to human trials. Health researchers hope it will make it possible to immunize large numbers of children and adults in Africa, Asia and South America efficiently and safely.

Scientists at the Michigan Nanotechnology Institute for Medicine and Biological Sciences at the University of Michigan [U-M] report that a novel, needleless method for getting an immunity-stimulating agent into the body has proved non-toxic and able to produce strong, sustained immune responses in animal studies. The vaccine is based on a super-fine emulsion of oil, water and surfactants [surface–tension-breaking substances] placed in the nose.

Nanotechnology Overcomes Obstacles

The nanoemulsion represents a new delivery method for an antigen already used in existing hepatitis B vaccines to activate the body's immune defenses.

"Our results indicate that needle-free nasal immunization, using a combination of nanoemulsion and hepatitis B antigen, could be a safe and effective hepatitis B vaccine, and also provide an alternative booster method for existing vaccines," says James R. Baker, Jr., M.D., the study's senior author and director of the institute. . . .

The nanoemulsion is made up of soybean oil, alcohol, water and detergents emulsified into droplets less than 400 nanometers in diameter.

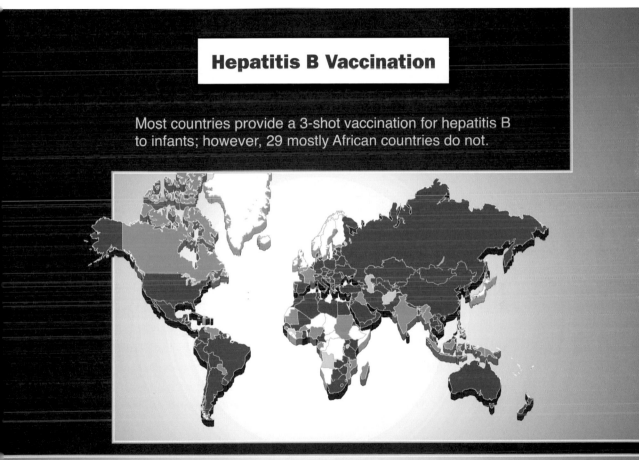

Hepatitis B Vaccination

Most countries provide a 3-shot vaccination for hepatitis B to infants; however, 29 mostly African countries do not.

164 countries introduced in national infant immunization schedule

 HepB3 ≥ 80% of infants immunized (131 countries or 68%)

HepB3 < 80% of infants immunized (30 countries or 15%)

HepB vaccine introduced but no coverage data reported (3 countries or 2%)

HepB* vaccine not introduced (29 countries or 15%)

*4 countries introduced HepB in *adolescent* immunization schedule

Taken from: WHO/UNICEF Coverage Estimates 1980–2006, August 2007.

The study suggests that the new type of hepatitis B vaccine will not have rigid cold storage requirements and could require fewer administrations than current vaccines, which require three shots given over a period of six months. Protective immunity with the new vaccine required only two immunizations in animals. The vaccine also avoids the risk of spreading needle-borne infections.

The nanoemulsion vaccine also avoids the temporary pain and redness that results after people get shots with the current vaccines, in which an irritating compound, alum, is used as an adjuvant, or enhancer of a vaccine's effect. There was no local inflammation at the nasal site of administration with the new vaccine.

This finding may be significant, because one of the major concerns for nasal administration of vaccines is that they can find their way to the olfactory bulb in the brain and cause side effects, says Paul E. Makidon, D.V.M., co–first author of the study and a U-M research fellow. "Our studies, however, indicate no inflammation and no evidence of the vaccine in the olfactory bulb," he says.

Baker's team has published earlier studies affirming the promise of nasal nanoemulsions as a strategy for smallpox, influenza, anthrax and HIV vaccines. The nanoemulsion technology is patented by U-M and licensed to Ann Arbor–based NanoBio Corporation. Baker is a founder and equity holder of NanoBio.

> **FAST FACT**
>
> According to the Hepatitis Foundation International, about 1 million people worldwide die each year from complications of hepatitis B.

Research on Animals Indicates Vaccine Is Safe

The research team determined effective doses of the antigen and nanoemulsion. In results obtained in mice, rats and guinea pigs, the nanoemulsion vaccine proved effective at producing three types of immunity: systemic, mucosal and cellular. Further toxicity studies in rodents and dogs showed the vaccine was safe and well-tolerated.

The vaccine was as effective as current hepatitis B vaccines in eliciting systemic protective antibodies in the blood of animals. The nanoemulsion acted as an effective adjuvant, without the need for a traditional adjuvant or inflammatory compound as in the current hepatitis B vaccines.

In addition, the nanoemulsion vaccine produced sustained cellular immunity in Th1 cells, which could make the vaccine useful in treating people with chronic hepatitis B whose own cellular immune responses are inadequate.

The animals given the nasal nanoemulsion in the study also activated a third type of immunity, mucosal immunity, which is gaining recognition among immunologists

A new vaccine developed using nanotechnology requires no refrigeration, making it easier to transport to third world countries fighting hepatitis B.
(AP Images)

as a key first-line response to infectious agents in diseases such as hepatitis B where mucosal tissues are involved in transmission. Baker and his team found the same effect of activating mucosal immunity that was seen in their previous studies of other nanoemulsion-based vaccines.

Moving the Vaccine to People Who Need It

The researchers tested whether the vaccine could remain stable and effective even if not refrigerated. They found the nanoemulsion vaccine retained its effectiveness for six months when kept at 25 degrees Celsius (77 degrees Fahrenheit), and even was stable and effective for six weeks at 40 degrees C (104 degrees F). This suggests that refrigeration will not be needed for the final distribution of the vaccine in developing countries, making it easier to vaccinate underserved people.

Current studies are focused on developing the pre-clinical data required to enter human trials, Baker says. The researchers hope that the first human trial can begin within a year.

2009 Update: The Gates Foundation–funded hepatitis B vaccine research at the University of Michigan was completed with favorable results. However, the Gates Foundation subsequently decided not to fund further stages, opting to fund a different vaccine project at the U-M.

Hepatitis C Is the Number One Reason for Liver Transplants

Peter Jaret

In the following viewpoint Peter Jaret says that more people require liver transplants due to the damaging effects of chronic hepatitis C than for any other reason. Advanced chronic hepatitis C can cause such serious scarring, or cirrhosis, that the liver can no longer function properly. If this happens, liver transplantation becomes the only viable option. Jaret provides an overview of the process people must go through in order to obtain a new liver, and what they must endure afterwards. According to Jaret, liver transplants are not a cure for hepatitis C. Typically, the disease returns and begins to damage the new liver. However, liver transplants have given many people with advanced hepatitis C disease, such as actor Larry Hagman and musician David Crosby, a second chance at life. Jaret is a contributing editor for *Health* magazine. His work has also appeared in *National Geographic*, *Newsweek*, *Hippocrates*, and many other national magazines.

SOURCE: Peter Jaret, "Hepatitis C and Liver Transplants," AHealthyMe.com, October 29, 2003. All contents copyright © 1999–2009 Blue Cross and Blue Shield of Massachusetts, Inc. Published with the permission of Consumer Health Interactive.

Most people know him as the bad guy JR Ewing on the TV show "Dallas." But lately the actor who played the part, Larry Hagman, has adopted a different role: champion for the cause of organ transplants.

Liver Transplants Provide a Second Chance

In 1995, Hagman, who had advanced cirrhosis, received a life-saving liver transplant. Since then he has gone on to become honorary chairman of the U.S. Transplant Games, an Olympics-style competition held for patients who have received donated organs. Hagman called the games "a true celebration of a second chance at life for transplant recipients from across the country."

For patients with advanced hepatitis C liver disease, liver transplants can offer just such a second chance. Cirrhosis of the liver caused by HCV [hepatitis C virus] infection is the leading reason for liver transplants. The surgery is complicated and can be risky. Yet it saves lives. About 73 to 77 percent of adult patients survive the operation and resume normal lives. Some 90 percent of liver transplants in children are successful. And new advances in the surgery, including the use of combination anti-viral therapy and "live donor" liver transplants, are improving those odds.

Among those who beat the odds is David Crosby, formerly of the band Crosby, Stills, Nash, and Young. Learning from doctors at Johns Hopkins in the 1990s that chronic hepatitis C had "munched" his liver "to a truly amazing degree . . . so that I had very little function left," he received a long-awaited liver transplant in 1994. Today, the grateful musician says he is "having a ball" raising a 3-year-old, touring with one of his sons, and making a documentary about musician activism. In his spare time, Crosby has also found time to narrate public service announcements about hepatitis C. "A lot of people think that if they ignore the disease, it will go away," he told an interviewer recently. "It won't. It will come knock on your door."

Not Everyone Qualifies for a Transplant

Because donated organs are in short supply, doctors carefully screen patients before putting them on the list to receive a liver.

In general, transplants are offered to patients who can't be treated using drugs or other therapies, and whose disease has become life-threatening. For HCV-infected patients, the most common reason for a transplant is severe cirrhosis, or scarring of the liver. Performing transplants on patients with liver cancer is less common and can be controversial. By the time cancer is detected, it has often spread too far to be cured by a liver transplant.

Surgeons transplant a liver into a recipient. Hepatitis C is the number one reason worldwide for liver transplants. (Michelle Del Guercio/ Photo Researchers, Inc.)

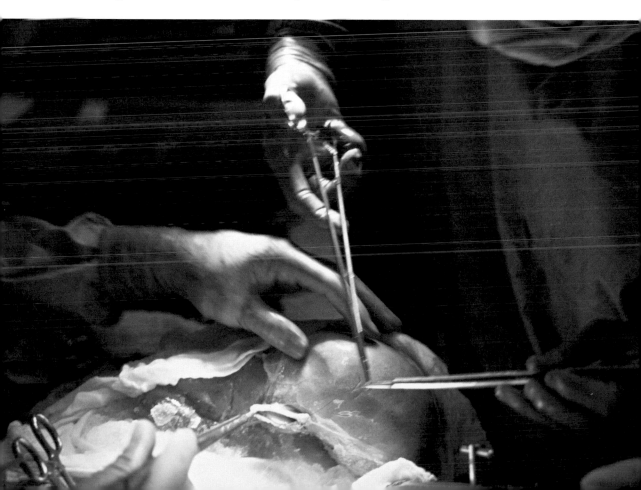

Transplants are usually not offered to people with ongoing drug or alcohol abuse problems, since the likelihood of success would be small. Crosby, for example, had experimented with needle drugs a few times and developed a serious drinking problem during his years on the road, but had been sober for 10 years before he learned he had hepatitis C. "I had already made the changes that I would recommend to anybody who discovers that they've got it, which are: Don't drink and don't use," he told Hep-C Alert. "I had decided that long before, or they wouldn't have done the treatment."

Timing is critical for patients who may need a liver transplant. Although transplantation is a last resort, it is important not to wait too long. If a patient's condition has seriously deteriorated, the chances of a successful liver transplant are lessened. Typically, a team from the liver transplant center determines, in consultation with the patient and family, whether a liver transplant is appropriate. Most centers have medical review boards that assess a patient's health information and make the final decision.

If a patient is approved, he or she is placed on the national waiting list for liver transplants. The wait can be a long one. It often takes more than a year to find a suitable donor.

Risks of Surgery

Like all major surgeries, liver transplants carry risks of infection and bleeding. During the surgery, doctors sometimes have difficulty removing the diseased liver. Problems can also arise if the blood vessels connected to the new liver develop clots, reducing blood supply to the transplanted organ. Once the surgery is completed, there is risk that the immune system will reject the organ. This danger can usually be minimized with drugs that suppress the rejection mechanism.

The chances of surviving a liver transplant vary depending on the age and condition of a patient. On aver-

Age of Liver Transplant Recipients in the United States, 2008

In 2008, a total of 27,958 Americans received liver transplants.

Age	Less than a year	1–5 years	6–10 years	11–17 years	18–34 years	35–49 years	50–64 years	65+ years
Number in age group	343	566	304	751	3,262	6,969	12,089	3,673
Percentage of total recipients	1%	2%	1%	2.7%	11.7%	25%	43%	13.2%

Taken from: Organ Procurement and Transplantation Network, U.S. Health Resources and Services Administration.

age, about three out of four transplant patients survive the first five years after transplantation. Those might not seem like very good odds. But among patients who are in good condition, the survival rate is as high as 90 percent. Among critically ill patients, the survival rate is about 50 percent.

Liver transplants are performed only at major medical centers around the country, by expert teams of transplantation surgeons. In the past, donated organs came only from people who had died and agreed to donate their organs. Recently some centers have also begun performing "live donor" organ transplants, in which part of the liver from a matched donor is removed and transplanted. The surgery is possible because healthy livers can regenerate themselves. Within a year, the part of the liver removed from a donor has fully grown back.

Transplant patients typically spend a few days in an intensive care unit after surgery, where their condition can be carefully monitored. Then they are moved to a regular hospital room for a stay of two to three weeks, on average. Patients who are critically ill at the time of the transplant may need to remain in intensive care and in the hospital longer, up to three months. Once patients leave intensive care, they begin to resume normal diets and are encouraged to get out of bed and walk.

The Paradox of Rejection

The most dangerous risk for transplantation patients is rejection. This occurs when the body's immune system attacks and destroys the transplanted organ.

Why does the immune system, which is there to protect us, try to reject the life-saving transplant? Rejection occurs because the immune system's job is to target and destroy foreign cells that pose a risk. Immune cells identify foreign cells by looking at unique molecular fingerprints on their surfaces and comparing them to the body's own unique molecular fingerprints. In this way, the immune system distinguishes between "self" and "non-self." A donor organ comes from someone whose cells have a different molecular fingerprint. Unfortunately, the immune system reacts as if the body has been invaded. It unleashes its destructive power to get rid of the foreign cells that it has mistakenly perceived as a threat. If not suppressed, the immune system can destroy a transplanted liver within days.

Several drugs have been developed that stop or slow the rejection process. Anti-rejection drugs may be given by injection during the first several weeks and later in pill form.

All anti-rejection drugs work by suppressing the immune system. As a result, they make patients more susceptible to infections. Other side effects include elevated blood pressure, fluid retention, puffiness, and bone loss. Over time, as the body begins to tolerate the new

> ## FAST FACT
>
> According to the American Liver Foundation, cirrhosis caused by hepatitis C is the most common reason for liver transplants.

organ, patients require less anti-rejection medicine. Still, it's likely that all transplant patients will have to take the drugs for the rest of their lives. Because of the potentially serious side effects, doctors typically try to lower the dosage to the smallest amount required to prevent rejection. To prevent serious infections, transplant patients are often given antibiotics in pill form.

Liver transplantation doesn't always succeed. In some cases, the transplanted organ may fail to function. Clots forming in the blood vessels that supply the transplanted organ may cut off blood supply, starving the new liver. Sometimes doctors are unable to stop the rejection process. If the liver begins to fail, a second transplant may be necessary.

For most patients, however, liver transplants are nothing short of a miracle. People who were seriously ill, like Crosby, have been able to return to full, active lives. Some, like snowboarder Chris Klug, compete in the US Transplant Games as a way to inspire other patients facing transplants. In July 2000, Klug received a liver transplant because of a rare congenital liver condition. Five months after the surgery he won a World Cup in the parallel giant slalom. He took home a bronze medal in the 2002 Winter Olympics.

New Advances Ahead

For HCV-positive patients, a liver transplant doesn't offer a cure. Because HCV is circulating in the bloodstream, the transplanted liver inevitably becomes infected with the virus. Over time, the infection can begin to injure the new liver.

Fortunately, advances in treating hepatitis C promise to slow that process dramatically. The higher the viral load at the time of surgery, studies have shown, the more quickly symptoms of hepatitis C infection recur in transplant patients. That finding led scientists to wonder if anti-viral treatments given before surgery could lower viral levels and protect the new liver from damage. To find out, experts at Loyola University Medical Center in Illinois have begun aggressively treating HCV patients with high doses of alpha interferon. Early results suggest that the treatment may help delay recurrence of the disease.

The use of "live donor" liver transplants, meanwhile, could significantly increase the availability of donor organs. Because this technique poses some risk to the healthy donor, however, it remains controversial. In 2002, the National Institutes of Health launched a seven-year study to assess the technique and identify the safest ways to perform the procedure.

Another new advance could help buy time for patients awaiting donor livers. The Mayo Clinic laboratory is developing a bioartificial liver, which operates outside the body like hemodialysis but contains live, functioning liver cells. This new form of therapy is intended not only for patients prior to transplantation but also for those in need of chronic supportive therapy.

CHAPTER 2

Controversies Surrounding Hepatitis

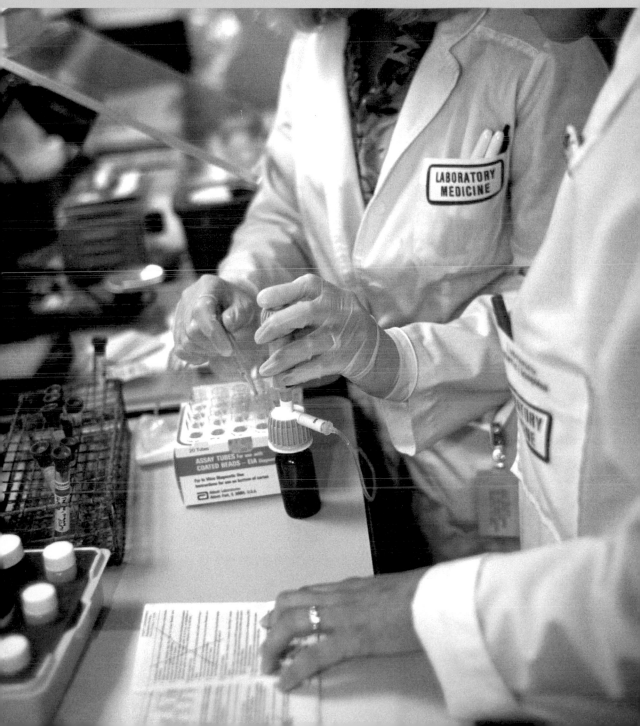

Treating Prisoners with Hepatitis C Is Cost Effective

Jennifer A. Tan, Tom A. Joseph, and Sammy Saab

In the following viewpoint Jennifer A. Tan, Tom A. Joseph, and Sammy Saab contend that treating hepatitis C in the U.S. prison population is cost effective. Treating hepatitis C–positive prisoners is a topic of debate because the treatment—a combination therapy consisting of pegylated interferon and ribavirin—is expensive and takes at least six months to a year to complete. Tan, Joseph, and Saab conducted a study using a common modeling approach called a Markov simulation to determine how much it would cost to treat prisoners with hepatitis C versus how much it would cost to care for them if they were not treated. The modeling results indicate that for most prisoners with hepatitis C, treatment with the combination therapy would cost less than the health care measures that would be required if the disease were allowed to progress to cirrhosis, cancer, or death. The authors contend that treatment should be offered to prisoners because it is cost effective. Tan, Joseph, and Saab are physicians and researchers in the Departments of Medicine and Surgery at the University of California at Los Angeles.

Photo on previous page. Lab workers perform a test for hepatitis B. (© Thomas Photography LLC/Alamy)

SOURCE: Jennifer A. Tan, Tom A. Joseph, and Sammy Saab, "Treating Hepatitis C in the Prison Population Is Cost-Saving," *Hepatology,* November 2008, pp. 1387–1395. Copyright © 2008 by John Wiley & Sons, Inc. All Rights Reserved. Reprinted by permission of John Wiley & Sons, Inc.

Hepatitis C infection is an important public health problem in the United States, with 1.3% of the population chronically infected with the virus. An even larger proportion of the U.S. prison population is affected, where the prevalence of chronic infection ranges from 12% to 31% [according to Anne Spaulding and other researchers], likely a result of increased rates of injection drug use within this group. Even more striking, approximately 29% to 43% of the total number of persons infected with hepatitis C in the United States pass through a correctional system each year [according to the U.S. Department of Justice (DOJ)].

As of midyear 2006, the U.S. prison system was continuing to grow in size, housing 2,245,189 inmates per year, or 497 per every 100,000 persons in the United States. The average length of incarceration has been increasing as well, placing a greater burden on prison health care systems to address chronic medical conditions such as hepatitis C. With the predicted cost of medical expenditures related to hepatitis C rising to as high as $10.7 billion from 2010 to 2019 [according to John Baak-shin Wong and colleagues], the U.S. prison health care system could see an estimated 15% to 60% increase in its budget in the coming years [according to the Centers for Disease Control and Prevention]. Consequently, the cost-effectiveness of hepatitis C treatment in prisons has been a matter of increasing public debate.

The Debate

Proponents of treatment in prisons argue that we have an ethical duty to provide prisoners with the contemporary best practices in medical care. They suggest that treatment of hepatitis C could be seamlessly integrated into existing programs that successfully manage tuberculosis, human immunodeficiency virus, and other transmittable diseases. Treatment could feasibly reduce the incidence of new hepatitis C virus (HCV) infections and prevent future complications from liver disease. Substance abuse and risk reduction counseling could be employed simultaneously, resulting in enduring benefits outside of prison.

Those who oppose treatment note that therapy is often interrupted by prison release or transfer, and that continued care for hepatitis C after release is often unavailable to what is a largely uninsured population. This could promote resistance to therapy or inadequate management of treatment-related adverse events. Furthermore, high rates of relapse to injection drug use or other high-risk activity result in considerable rates of reinfection after prison release, which could be expected to undermine the benefits of treatment.

Prior studies have demonstrated that treatment of chronic hepatitis C with pegylated interferon (PEG IFN) and ribavirin is a cost-effective measure in the general population. However, no study has yet addressed whether combination therapy would be cost-effective in the prison population. This study aims to answer this question in the male prison population, which makes up 87.3% of the inmate population.

Study Strategy

We conducted a MEDLINE search of the published literature using various combinations of the search terms "hepatitis C," "treatment," "cost-effectiveness," "prisons," "pegylated-interferon and ribavirin," "combination therapy," "jails," and "inmates."

Using data obtained from these articles, we used the software Treeage Pro Health Module to construct a decision analysis model employing Markov simulation. This allowed us to estimate the incremental cost-effectiveness ratio (ICER) of combination therapy for hepatitis C in the U.S. prison population and thus compare the strategy of treatment to that of no treatment. The perspective adopted was that of the U.S. prison health care system. We

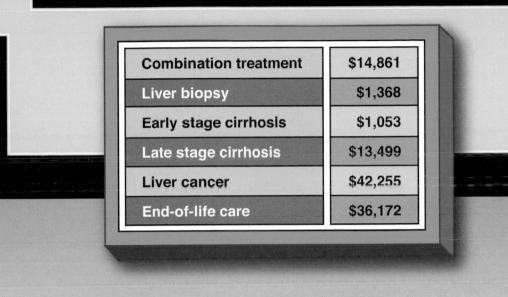

Hepatitis C–Related Costs per Year per Prisoner in the U.S. Prison Population, 2007

Combination treatment	$14,861
Liver biopsy	$1,368
Early stage cirrhosis	$1,053
Late stage cirrhosis	$13,499
Liver cancer	$42,255
End-of-life care	$36,172

Taken from: Jennifer A. Tan, Tom A. Joseph, and Sammy Saab, "Treating Hepatitis C in the Prison Population Is Cost-Saving," *Hepatology*, November 2008.

used the generally accepted cost-effectiveness threshold of $50,000 per quality-adjusted life years (QALYs) as the maximum value for determining the preferred treatment option.

The target population at the beginning of our analysis was a cohort [group] of men, ages 40 to 49 years, who were incarcerated in the U.S. prison system and chronically infected with hepatitis C. . . . Their baseline demographics were assumed to be similar to that of the general U.S. prison population. In a bulletin published by the Bureau of Justice in May 2006, Caucasians comprised the largest proportion of prisoners at 44.3%, followed by African Americans at 38.9% and Latinos at 15%. Men were 7 times more likely to be imprisoned than females, and comprised 87.3% of the prison population. The average age of the prisoners was 41 ± 7 years. These

demographics were consistent with the inmate populations studied in the published literature we used to make
baseline assumptions for our model.

We presumed that genotype [genetic makeup] determination was performed in all prisoners prior to com-
mencement of therapy. The inmates were accorded a
distribution of genotypes as reported in the literature
specific to the prison population: 78% were assumed to
have genotype 1, and 22% were assumed to have genotypes 2 and 3. . . .

Two strategies were then analyzed. In the first strategy, prisoners did not undergo a liver biopsy prior to starting treatment. They were assumed to have a distribution
of stages of fibrosis [damage to the liver] in accordance
with the literature. . . .

In the second strategy, all prisoners underwent a liver
biopsy prior to beginning therapy in order to determine
their stage of fibrosis. . . .

Results Demonstrate Cost-Effectiveness

Our results demonstrate that PEG IFN and ribavirin combination therapy is cost-effective in the prison
population, both in strategies with and without biopsy.
Incorporating a pretreatment liver biopsy may be the
most cost-effective approach, however, as one could potentially exclude certain patients with no fibrosis from
therapy. Although we had not expected treatment to be
cost-effective because of the high reinfection rates and
nonliver mortality rates both inside and outside prison,
treatment remained cost-effective despite varying these
factors over wide ranges.

The only segment of the prison population in which
treatment was not cost-effective was incarcerated individuals between the ages of 40 and 49 with genotype 1
and no fibrosis. Given their age and lack of liver damage,
they have a lower probability than other groups of developing cirrhosis and hepatic decompensation [a decrease

in liver function]. Their disease process is largely silent, their quality of life is relatively unaffected, and they are more likely to die from non-liver-related causes. . . .

No Standard Policy

Currently, we are not aware of a standard policy on the treatment of U.S. prisoners with chronic hepatitis C. Even screening for hepatitis C infection remains controversial and is not universally performed. As of 2000, 1,209 of 1,584 state public and private adult correctional facilities, housing 94% of all state prisoners, reported that they tested inmates for hepatitis C; 1,104 (70%) state correctional facilities reported that they had some type of policy for treating hepatitis C in their inmates. Between July 1, 1999, and June 30, 2000, 4,750 inmates were treated for hepatitis C.

A California prison inmate consults with a prison physician. The authors say that treating prisoners with hepatitis would cost less than the expenditures resulting from providing health care until death. (AP Images)

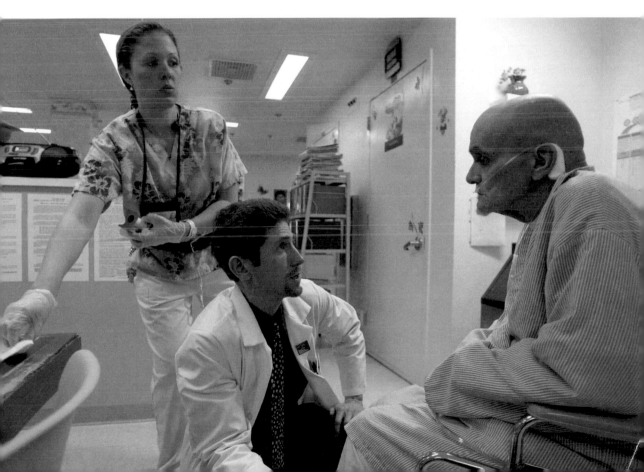

Policies vary widely from state to state, however. In some states, written protocols exist for the treatment of prisoners, and in others, selection for treatment is performed on a case-by-case basis. In certain states, liver biopsy is mandatory prior to treatment, and in others, the decision to biopsy is left to health care providers. A minimum prison sentence of 15 to 18 months is required by many states in order to assure completion of treatment and adequate follow-up prior to release. A minority of states do not have any established programs for hepatitis C treatment.

> ## FAST FACT
>
> According to the Centers for Disease Control and Prevention, HCV infection is most prevalent among people born between 1945 and 1965.

In order to address this issue, the Federal Bureau of Prisons put forth a set of clinical practice guidelines in 2005. They recommend that treatment be continued in prisoners who are already on therapy and that therapy be initiated in prisoners who meet criteria published by the American Association for the Study of Liver Diseases, provided that they do not have contraindications such as severe psychiatric or medical illness. Prisoners must also demonstrate a commitment to abstinence from alcohol and other substances. Genotyping is suggested for all patients, and liver biopsy is suggested for patients with elevated alanine aminotransferase levels, genotype 1, or suspected compensated cirrhosis. The Bureau recommends that treatment not be initiated in short-term inmates, given the high likelihood that therapy will not be completed. Enforcement of such a national guideline is problematic, however, because there is currently no centrally funded or administered program to employ hepatitis C treatment. Each state manages its own budget and therefore adopts its own set of treatment guidelines.

Ethical Considerations

Ethical considerations also play a large role in this matter of public controversy, and the cost-effectiveness of treatment must be weighed against these other concerns. As with liver transplantation, proponents of treatment argue that it is unconstitutional to deny inmates access to treatment that is considered standard care. In 2003, Oregon inmates filed a class-action lawsuit against the state prison system, alleging cruel and unusual punishment, and sought $17.5 million in medical expenses, drug therapy, and potential liver transplantations. A settlement was reached in 2004, resulting in liberalization of the state's hepatitis C treatment guidelines, and was considered by many to be a victory in favor of treatment.

Those who oppose therapy for prisoners, however, maintain that incarcerated individuals, by virtue of their offenses, have forfeited their right to receive these resources, particularly as treatment would be administered at the expense of taxpayers, while a large proportion of uninsured patients continue to be denied access to therapy.

Treatment Should Not Be Withheld

If the decision to treat is based on pharmaco-economic measures, however, the results of our analysis suggest that treatment is cost-saving and should not be withheld in U.S. prisoners with hepatitis C. Because the efficacy treatment is diminished by relapse of injection drug use and reinfection, this treatment strategy must be coupled with educational and substance abuse programs. Furthermore, because mental illness is widespread in the prison population and can often be exacerbated by treatment, careful mental health screening and follow-up would be required.

In conclusion, although the ethical debate regarding the implementation of treatment for hepatitis C in prisons is not likely to be settled soon, we can assert that from a pharmaco-economic standpoint, treatment of hepatitis C in the prison population is cost-effective.

Treating All Prisoners with Hepatitis C May Not Be Feasible

Owen J. Murray, John Pulvino, Jacques Baillargeon, David Paar, and Ben G. Raimer

In the following viewpoint Owen J. Murray, John Pulvino, Jacques Baillargeon, David Paar, and Ben G. Raimer contend that it is impossible for prisons to treat all hepatitis C–positive prisoners. According to the authors, it is impractical to provide hepatitis C treatment to prisoners with short sentences and to those whose disease is asymptomatic. They say that since the standard hepatitis C treatment takes six months to a year to complete, only those prisoners with sufficiently long sentences should be treated. Additionally, the authors say, since prison health care budgets are small and hepatitis C treatment is expensive, treatment should be offered only to those prisoners who will clearly benefit. The authors say that managing hepatitis C in the prison system presents many challenges to prison health care providers. Murray, Pulvino, Baillargeon, Paar, and Raimer are physicians or researchers affiliated with the Correctional Managed Care program at the University of Texas Medical Branch at Galveston.

SOURCE: Owen J. Murray, John Pulvino, Jacques Baillargeon, David Paar, and Ben G. Raimer, "Managing Hepatitis C in Our Prisons: Promises and Challenges," *CorrectCare,* Spring 2007. Reproduced by permission.

America's prisons and jails bear a disproportionate share of the total U.S. population infected with HCV [hepatitis C virus]. Epidemiologic studies show that the prevalence of HCV infection in correctional facilities (15% to 40%) is significantly higher than that for the general population (1.6%). Translated into actual numbers, these prevalence rates suggest that between 300,000 and 400,000 HCV-infected persons are incarcerated in U.S. prisons or jails at any point in time.

Since the vast majority of these individuals will eventually be released into the community, the degree to which correctional health care providers are able to control and manage this infectious disease has enormous public health implications.

Prisons Face Enormous Challenges in Dealing with Hepatitis C

Prevalence data suggest that at least one-third of all HCV-infected persons in the United States pass through a correctional facility in any given year. Consequently, some health policy analysts have argued that prison systems are optimal venues for implementing comprehensive HCV prevention and medical management programs because they can efficiently target a high concentration of infected persons.

Unfortunately, most correctional institutions are confronting unprecedented challenges in their attempts to address the growing HCV epidemic. These challenges primarily revolve around financial and logistical impediments to evaluating and treating such a large number of patients, as well as the absence of a clear consensus about how to best manage the disease in the unique environment of a prison.

A related challenge is the general scarcity of follow-up care available in the community once an inmate with HCV is released. The Texas prison system, which holds one of the largest groups of HCV-infected inmates in the

The high rate of tattooing in prisons has spawned a near epidemic of hepatitis, due to the use of dirty needles and other unsanitary procedures. (AP Images)

nation, offers an illustrative snapshot of both the promises and challenges of managing HCV in the correctional environment.

Texas Prison System Illustrative of Challenges

The Texas Department of Criminal Justice (TDCJ) houses more than 153,000 convicted inmates in prison units, state jails and substance abuse felony punishment facilities. A recent seroprevalence survey of nearly 4,000 adults entering a TDCJ facility showed that about 29% of the new inmates were HCV positive. This finding suggests that more than 40,000 inmates in the custody of TDCJ may be infected with the virus.

All medical, dental and psychiatric care for TDCJ inmates is provided by two of the state's academic medical centers. Evaluating and caring for a cohort [group] of HCV-infected inmates that is larger than the total population of most state prison systems has proved to be a daunting task, requiring health care providers to do more with less in the face of soaring medical costs and finite government funding.

Targeted Screening

To identify inmates who are HCV-positive, TDCJ uses voluntary serologic screening targeted at inmates with risk factors for the infection (e.g., history of injection drug use, known HIV scropositivity or high-risk sexual activity). Although some infectious disease experts advocate universal HCV screening, such an approach is probably not cost-effective and would likely decimate the health care budgets of many prison systems.

Approximately 20,000 HCV-positive inmates in TDCJ have been identified and are being managed by a network of medical professionals.

All newly diagnosed inmates undergo a comprehensive medical evaluation by a physician or midlevel provider. They also receive extensive education about the disease process, medical management and treatment options, and methods to prevent transmission of the virus and minimize disease progression.

Asymptomatic patients with an elevated alanine aminotransferase (ALT) level but no laboratory evidence of advanced liver disease are monitored and undergo repeat ALT testing at three-month intervals for the first 12 to 15 months after diagnosis.

Symptomatic patients are typically enrolled in a chronic care clinic where their condition can be more closely monitored during the initial evaluation period. Criteria for selecting potential candidates for antiviral therapy are based on clinical practice guidelines formulated by an internal pharmacy and therapeutics committee comprised of health care professionals from TDCJ and the two medical centers. These guidelines mirror national consensus recommendations but are tailored to accommodate the special circumstances of managing chronic HCV infection in a large prison system.

Limited Treatment Is the Only Choice

Combination therapy with pegylated interferon and ribavirin represents a major advance in the management of hepatitis C, with an overall sustained virologic response rate of 40% to 50%. Successful eradication of the virus eliminates the potential for HCV transmission and prevents or significantly delays further liver damage and associated complications. Unfortunately, correctional health care providers are able to provide antiviral therapy to only a minority of the HCV-infected inmates due to several unresolved stumbling blocks.

Because of the amount of time required for evaluation and treatment of HCV, a major determinant of eligibility for antiviral therapy in the correctional setting is the expected duration of an inmate's incarceration. Most inmates who are released are uninsured and cannot afford to pay for costly medical services. And with few exceptions, public health agencies do not have the resources to provide treatment for the indigent HCV population in the community.

This harsh reality has left correctional health administrators with little choice other than to exclude inmates with short sentences from consideration for antiviral therapy since partial treatment provides little clinical benefit and is an inefficient use of limited resources. The effects of this policy are especially profound for HCV-infected inmates in state jails and other short-term detention facilities since few if any of them are eligible for treatment.

Cost is another major obstacle to providing treatment for HCV-infection. Antiviral therapy is expensive, with recent estimates for a course of treatment ranging from a low of $7,000 to a high of $20,000. Correctional health care is paid for almost entirely by government appropriations, which typically do not provide sufficient funds for managing the large numbers of inmates with

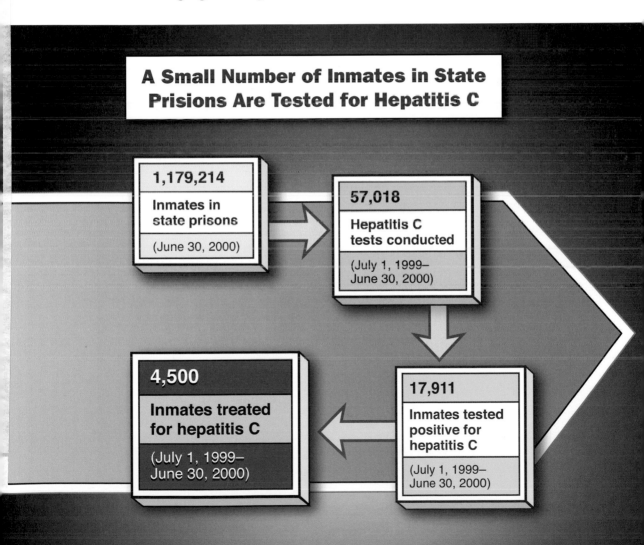

A Small Number of Inmates in State Prisons Are Tested for Hepatitis C

1,179,214
Inmates in state prisons
(June 30, 2000)

57,018
Hepatitis C tests conducted
(July 1, 1999–June 30, 2000)

4,500
Inmates treated for hepatitis C
(July 1, 1999–June 30, 2000)

17,911
Inmates tested positive for hepatitis C
(July 1, 1999–June 30, 2000)

Taken from: U.S. Bureau of Justice Statistics, Hepatitis Testing and Treatment in State Prisons, April 2004, and Prison and Jail Inmates at Mid-Year 2000, March 2001.

HCV. Consequently, providers have had little choice but to limit antiviral therapy to those patients who are most likely to benefit from treatment.

Lowering Hepatitis C–Related Costs

Between September 2005 and August 2006, more than 300 TDCJ inmates completed a course of combination therapy with interferon and ribavirin. Treatment for this sizeable group of patients was possible because of several aggressive initiatives to control costs. These include the use of clinical protocols and case management strategies to reduce the inappropriate use of expensive resources while improving overall clinical outcomes.

Telemedicine has also proved to be an effective strategy for reducing costs associated with HCV treatment. Because most TDCJ units are in rural areas, telemedicine enables specialty providers to monitor patients remotely for potentially serious side effects during the course of antiviral therapy.

The most significant savings in treating HCV-infected inmates have been achieved through the participation of one of the medical centers (University of Texas Medical Branch) in the 340B Drug Pricing Program. Created under the Veterans Health Care Act of 1992, this program provides substantial discounts on covered outpatient drugs (including antiviral medications) purchased by federally funded entities serving the most vulnerable patient populations.

Paying for Liver Transplants Would Drain Health Care Budgets

Chronic HCV infection is now the leading cause of end-stage liver disease (ESLD) in TDCJ and other state prison systems, and more cases of liver failure are expected as

> **FAST FACT**
>
> According to a 2002 article in the *American Journal of Public Health,* 50 to 80 percent of new injection drug users become infected with hepatitis C within six to twelve months of their initial injection.

the number of elderly inmates continues to rise. The cost of managing variceal bleeding, hepatic encephalopathy and other serious complications of liver failure is substantial.

Approximately 300 inmates with ESLD are currently incarcerated in Texas prisons. Ultimately, the only viable treatment for some of these patients will be liver transplantation. The enormous costs of liver transplantation and long-term immunosuppressive therapy are staggering and have the potential to consume most, if not all, of many correctional health care budgets.

The ethical and legal issues of providing organ transplants to prisoners have been contentiously debated for more than a decade. Thus far, only a handful of state and federal prisoners have received organ transplants. However, since organ transplantation is now an accepted standard of care and as the federal courts have begun to address the constitutionality of denying inmates access to such treatment, the number of inmates with ESLD who qualify for placement on a transplant waiting list is expected to gradually increase. Organ transplantation may very well represent the most significant financial challenge that correctional health care systems have ever had to confront.

Challenges of Chronic Bloodborne Diseases

The current challenge of managing hepatitis C in our prisons is comparable to the problems faced by correctional programs during the early days of the HIV epidemic. Comprehensive guidelines for identifying and treating HCV-infected inmates are still evolving, and expensive antiviral therapy remains a major obstacle. Nonetheless, correctional health care has successfully met the challenges of a chronic, bloodborne infectious disease before, and there is every reason to believe that cost-effective, systematic approaches to the HCV epidemic are attainable.

Health Care Workers Should Be Tested for Hepatitis C

David M. Sine

In the following viewpoint David M. Sine argues that health care workers (HCW) should be routinely tested for hepatitis C. According to Sine, the risks of hepatitis C transmission from an infected HCW to a patient are documented and significant. Because of these risks, Sine believes HCWs have an ethical duty to be tested for hepatitis C and to inform prospective patients of their hepatitis C status. Many HCWs avoid hepatitis C testing for fear of the ramifications to their careers of a positive result. The author believes that testing all HCWs before they are hired by hospitals and other health care organizations would benefit both HCWs and patients: HCWs would be given a chance to proactively manage a serious disease, and patients would be allowed to make informed decisions about their care. Sine refutes arguments that requiring HCW testing for hepatitis C is an invasion of privacy. Sine is the senior staff engineer for the Joint Commission on Accreditation of Healthcare Organizations and a senior consultant for the American Hospital Association.

SOURCE: David M. Sine, "Testing for Hepatitis C in Healthcare Workers Prior to a Known Occupational Exposure: A Reconsideration," *Journal of SH & E Research,* vol. 5, Spring 2008. © 2008 American Society of Safety Engineers. Reproduced by permission.

N
ational policies regarding the testing of healthcare workers for transmissible blood borne pathogens have changed little since issued by the CDC [Centers for Disease Control and Prevention] in 1991 and no current federal policy recommends the testing of healthcare workers prior to an occupational exposure to hepatitis C laden blood. The research and discussion of this paper will support the inclusion of testing for hepatitis C (HCV) as a part of the post offer, pre-placement physical for healthcare workers (HCW) in a hospital setting. Current law does not require testing and some laws, such as the ADA [Americans with Disabilities Act] or the Fair Housing and Employment Act, may actually discourage determination of HCV status as a part of a healthcare worker employee pre-employment physical.

This paper will briefly review and reject three of the most commonly advanced arguments against the testing of healthcare workers: risk of exposure, informed consent and/or duty to warn, and employee privacy. The benefits to HCWs, patients, and employers provided by a rejection of these three arguments are described and a policy of routine pre-exposure HCV testing is proposed.

Prevalence of HCV in the General Population

At present, over 4 million Americans have HCV antibodies of which about 2.7 million have active hepatitis C virus infection (HCV prevalence in the general population is estimated to be 1.6% to 1.8%). Compared with an estimate of about 750,000 Americans infected with HIV hepatitis C is a far more prevalent disease. There are 25,000 new HCV infections reported every year: HCV is the most common chronic blood borne infection in the United States and the most frequently reported viral infection in Canada. There are 170 million cases worldwide.

Progression to chronic liver disease and other complications make end-stage liver disease due to HCV the most common underlying cause for liver transplantation in the United States. HCV, attributable for 8,000 to 10,000 deaths per year, is the 10th leading cause of death in the United States. 85% of those infected will develop chronic infection; however, the disease process is slow and it can take as many as 20 years for the disease to present symptoms in some victims. 70% of all chronic cases will develop liver disease and the Association for Professionals in Infection Control and Epidemiology (APIC) states that HCWs account for 2% to 4% of known acute cases.

Transmission of the infection can be caused by exposure to infected blood, blood products, shared IV needles, shared tattoo needles, and through unprotected sex. . . .

Prevalence of HCV in the Healthcare Worker (HCW)

HCW and emergency medical and public safety workers, such as firefighters or police officers, are at significant occupational risk of exposure to HCV. The CDC estimates that two out of every 100 healthcare workers will be infected with HCV after a needlestick or a similar type of exposure to HCV positive blood in the workplace. A statistical study of 10,654 HCW in Scotland in 2001 indicated an overall rate of HCV infection of .28% (30/10,654) with sub group rates of 1.4% for surgeons and 1% for physicians. . . .

In general, the prevalence of HCV infection in HCWs is assumed to be the same or even slightly less than that of the general population; however, certain sub-groups of healthcare workers, such as surgeons, have a higher rate of infection than the general population.

Current Standards Are Conflicting

The current standards do not require nor do they recommend mandatory testing of HCWs prior to a known work related exposure. However, current standards do

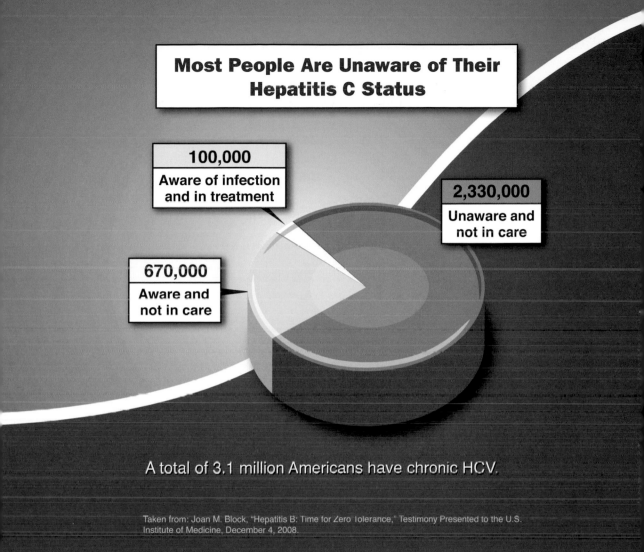

Most People Are Unaware of Their Hepatitis C Status

100,000
Aware of infection and in treatment

2,330,000
Unaware and not in care

670,000
Aware and not in care

A total of 3.1 million Americans have chronic HCV.

Taken from: Joan M. Block, "Hepatitis B: Time for Zero Tolerance," Testimony Presented to the U.S. Institute of Medicine, December 4, 2008.

clearly suggest that HCWs learn their own health status and take appropriate actions. In 2006, as in 1991, mandatory testing for blood borne pathogens is not recommended by CDC but it remained a suggested ethical obligation of HCWs performing exposure prone procedures to know their health status and self report to the profession's regulatory body. Only if a HCW is determined to be HCV positive after an occupational exposure is a review of the high risk clinical procedures in which that particular HCW is likely to be engaged recommended to prevent HCW to patient transmission of blood borne pathogens. No practice restrictions are recommended between the time of the potential exposure to HCV laden blood and the determination of the HCW's HCV status.

This presents a conflict for employer and employee (HCW) alike: how (and when) to determine HCV status in the absence of pre-exposure HCV testing. This dichotomy in recommendation is seen when comparing the typical statements of authorities having jurisdiction based upon the most recent CDC recommendations. The resulting conflict between recommendations given by state health departments is typified by the following recommendations from the Department of Health from the state of Michigan:

> Routine or mandatory HIV, HBV, and HCV testing of all HCWs *is not recommended*, nor should it be a requirement for employment, credentialing, licensure, or insurance.

> HCWs *are encouraged to be aware* of their HIV, HBV, and HCV serologic status and seek treatment to *reduce the risk of transmission* [of] blood-borne pathogens to sexual contacts and patients through unanticipated occupational exposures. (*emphasis added*)

Since the latency period of HCV is so long and the appearance of symptoms can be delayed for months if not years, in the absence of routine testing the HCW may not be aware of their serologic status [positive or negative status with respect to a particular antibody, such as HIV] and thus not in compliance with these vague recommendations for self testing.

The above two statements beg the question: If healthcare workers (or certain sub-groups of healthcare workers) are at a greater risk of being and having been exposed to HCV than that of the general public, should not HCWs be routinely tested for HCV (as is only suggested by the second statement) and not wait, as is the current practice, until after a known and documented workplace exposure as a means to better protect themselves and their patients?

Risk of Transmission Not Insignificant

Pre-employment testing of HCWs for HCV would serve two significant purposes: alerting HCWs to their health status so that they may seek treatment and counseling, and to reduce the risk of HCW to patient HCV transmission through appropriate use of personal protective equipment and practice restrictions.

Many arguments against the inclusion of HCV testing in a HCW pre-employment physical cite the low risk of transmission of HCV from HCW to patient. The risk of transmission from a HCW infected with a blood borne pathogen infection to a patient is often described by those opposed to pre-employment testing as either small, remote, low, extremely low, or rare. It is further argued that the risk, cost, and potential liability of pre-employment HCV testing returns insufficient benefit when placed in balance with the risk of HCW to patient transmission. Physician [R. Stefan Ross and colleagues] have suggested in a 2002 study that the risk of a surgeon (gynecologist) with known HCV infection transmitting HCV to their patients is as low as one in 1,750 operations.

In reality, the risk of HCW to patient transmission is not yet fully understood. However, more recent studies and events are beginning to give a better picture of the risk and how it should be better managed. A more recent study concluded that a HCV positive cardiac surgeon transmitted HCV to as many as 14 of 937 patients (1.5 % or 1500:100,000).

Since the 1991 CDC recommendations were issued there have been 132 documented HCW to patient transmissions of blood borne pathogens, 38 of which were HCV related. Various retrospective studies of these nosocomial [hospital acquired] infections have placed the rate of transmission from HCW to patient during invasive procedures as high as 2.25%. While the above referenced

> **FAST FACT**
>
> The Centers for Disease Control and Prevention estimates that chronic HCV infection causes eight thousand to ten thousand deaths each year in the United States.

study of the HCV positive Long Island cardiac surgeon's patients for a ten year interval produced a rate of 1.5%, the risk of transmission may be influenced by type and duration of procedure as well as technique within the procedure, experience of the surgeon, and fatigue.

Putting Risks in Perspective

The most common site of exposure for physicians is still the OR [operating room] yet operating room physicians have the lowest level of compliance in reporting their injuries, obviously a significant confounding factor for the available data. As an example of underreporting, an anesthesiologist was diagnosed as having acute hepatitis C three days after providing anesthesia during the thoracotomy [chest incision] of a 64-year-old man. Eight weeks later that patient was diagnosed as having acute hepatitis C. None of the surgical team, including the anesthesiologist, recalls any unusual events or incidents (e.g. needle stick injuries) that occurred during the patient's procedure and no incident reports were filed. Clearly, current infection control practices and the use of personal protective equipment is not failsafe.

It is important to place these estimates of risk of HCV positive HCW to patient transmission in perspective by comparing them to other risks that garner much more public and regulatory concern. As of 2001, the risk of HCV infection from a unit of transfused blood is less than one per million transfused units. The estimated risk of HIV transmission during unprotected sex varies greatly but a common figure often cited is 1:100,000 for male to female and 1:200,000 for female to male. The risk for HCV transmission from a HCW to a patient (1500:100,000) is significantly higher than these comparative evidence based estimates referenced above.

The real question then becomes: by what reasonable ethical standard can these risks of HCW to patient transmission be considered so low that the healthcare community has no ethical duty to determine HCW health status and to warn patients of their risk during treatment? It remains an undisputed fact that the risk of transmission from a HCW to a patient is only zero in a HCW who is not HCV positive. Also undisputed is that the known risk of transmission is thought to be greater today than when the current standard was developed; the standards, therefore, should be strengthened accordingly.

"Don't Ask and Don't Tell" Does Not Work

In an article published in JAMA [*Journal of the American Medical Association*] in 2000, [Larry] Gostin concluded that there is no duty to inform a patient of a HCW's serological health status. This is similar to the promulgated standards (recommendations) of the CDC which have been reinforced by public statements made by CDC executive leadership. It is also believed that by revealing serostatus, that the HCW potentially places at risk their professional career due to practice restriction and stigmatization. Because of these fears, many HCWs do not attempt to discover their HCV serologic status and assume that by not doing so they then have no duty to warn patients. However, the duty of a physician to warn a patient of their positive serostatus is established by [court] cases such as Faya, Behringer and Kerins and patients have clearly indicated that they consider it well within their right (of informed consent) to know the serostatus of their healthcare providers. . . .

The current practice of "don't ask and don't tell," however, places both the HCW and the patient at risk. By not determining their HCV status, the HCW potentially and needlessly delays the start of treatment of an insidious disease with a long latency period. By not communicating a seropositve status to a patient, the HCW denies the patient one of the pillars of informed consent: the actual known risks of a clinical procedure.

Recent surveys of patient attitudes support the need to include patient notification of HCW serostatus *before* a medical procedure commences as a "central value" of the healthcare profession. In a recent study involving U.S. households (2,353 respondents), 89% agreed that they would want to know if their dentist or doctor was infected with HCV and 82% agreed that disclosure of HBV or HCV infection in a provider should be mandatory. Clearly, if central values of a profession are determined by a dialog between members of a profession and the community that the profession serves, then notification of patients of HCW serostatus is to be included as a component of informed consent.

Duty to Inform

The duty to warn patients that may be or may have been exposed to a blood borne pathogen is clearly established in the informed consent process for blood transfusion as well as the national look-back programs for previous exposures to potentially HCV laden blood or blood products. In both examples, the patient is informed of the potential for infection (and in the [latter] encouraged to seek testing and, if indicated, treatment).

Case law may also support the conclusion that both the hospital and the HCW have a duty to warn if there is a risk of unintended (and preventable) transmission of a (blood borne) disease to a third party. The Corpus Christi Court of Appeals in *Garcia v. Santa Rosa Healthcare Corp.* held that healthcare professionals "who discover some disease or medical condition which their services or products have likely caused" owe a duty to warn a third party. In our application of this finding to our issue, the HCW and hospital owe that duty to a patient so that an unnamed third party at risk such as children or a sexual partner may be notified or protected.

There is existing language in some state regulations that addresses the duty to warn in the case of other blood borne pathogens. The following language, adapted from the State of Michigan Department of Health, is typical:

> If an infected health-care worker's serostatus becomes known, a notification of patient(s) should be considered on a case-by-case basis.

Still, the CDC only recommends that HCWs be tested only after a known exposure (e.g. needle sticks or splashes to the eye) to HCV-positive blood. A significant difference between the HCW and the patient is that the HCW generally knows that they have been exposed and can seek testing and treatment. Not so the patient . . . no statutory provision exists that compels the HCW to inform the patient so that they may seek testing and treatment if an unintended exposure to blood occurs while in the care of a HCW. Thus, patients are not given the same opportunity as HCWs to be tested, seek early pre-symptomatic treatment, or to alter personal behaviors that may place sexual partners or children at risk.

The current national policy of not testing HCWs and, therefore, not informing patients as a part of the consent process offers no reduction of risk to either patients or HCWs. The next question then becomes is the pre-employment test for HCV status of an HCW an invasion of privacy and, if so, does the right of privacy prevent the routine testing of the HCW for HCV serostatus?

Privacy Arguments Do Not Hold Up

The privacy arguments against mandatory pre-employment testing of HCV serostatus take two tracks: first, that the health status of a HCW is of no concern to the patient and to reveal serostatus is a violation of HCW expectation for privacy, and, second, that the test itself is an invasion of HCW privacy.

If the first argument is valid then it must be applied to more than only HCV status. However, the current CDC requirements do require that the HIV status of a HCW be disclosed before performing exposure-prone procedures. As previously discussed in the above section, disclosure has become a cultural, ethical and legal expectation. In many states the standard of care (and case law) requires that HCWs disclose risks that a "reasonable patient" would want to know. These norms should apply equally to all blood borne pathogens including HIV, HBV, and HCV.

The second argument, that the test itself is an invasion of privacy, also fails when compared to current practices to test HCWs for other communicable diseases and to vaccinate against them. HCWs are required by law to submit to annual TB [tuberculosis] tests, annual vaccinations against influenza and HBV, and similar invasions of person and privacy to prevent or limit the spread of communicable disease in the public interest.

To not test and appropriately disclose the serostatus of a HCW creates asymmetrical policies in these matters of privacy as the HCV status of the patient is routinely probed and noted by the HCW. The CDC recommends that physicians routinely question their patients concerning risk factors for (HCV) infection.

How can it be ethical for some [to] claim a right to privacy that others may not similarly claim when that right has been set aside specifically to benefit the public good and health as is the case in mandatory vaccinations? The only available reasonable conclusion must be that such arbitrary claims of invasion of privacy are inconsistent and neither ethical nor in keeping with applicable case law.

Conclusions: HCWs Should Be Tested Before Employment

Current standards regarding the pre-employment testing of HCWs are not consistent with those that apply to other blood born pathogens and communicable diseases. In application, this policy produces infection control practices that are asymmetrical and place the patient at a disadvantage in both the informed consent process and in the

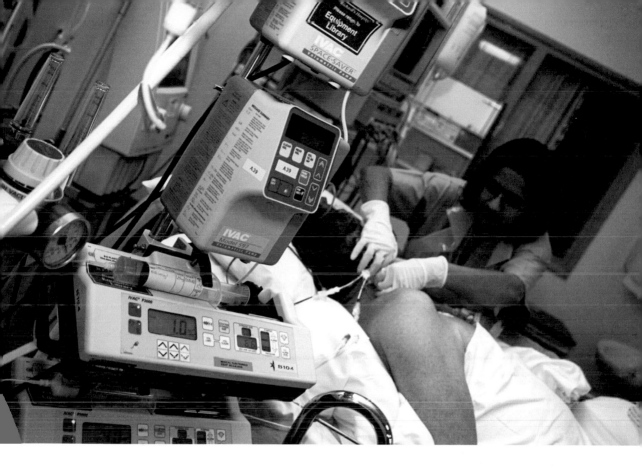

management of their personal health. A more aggressive approach to testing, in keeping with the recent change in the recommended testing protocol for HIV by the CDC and our growing understanding of the risk of HCV transmission, is now needed. Without unfettered access by HCWs to their serostatus, and without knowledge of HCWs' serostatus by patients, little else can be done to mitigate and manage the inadvertent but apparently inevitable percutaneous transmission of hepatitis C. The author concludes that HCW behavior regarding voluntary testing or inclusion of HCV serostatus as a part of an informed consent process will not change until the current standards for HCV pre-placement testing are modified, adopted, and enforced by authorities having jurisdiction such as CMS [Centers for Medicare and Medicaid Services], JCAHO [Joint Commission on Accreditation of Healthcare Organizations] and state health departments.

The author argues that health care workers should be tested for hepatitis C prior to being hired by a health care facility, to protect patients from infection. (John Cole/Photo Researchers, Inc.)

Health Care Workers Should Not Be Tested for Hepatitis C

Bashyr Aziz

In the following viewpoint Bashyr Aziz argues against United Kingdom (UK) Department of Health (DH) guidelines requiring the testing of new nursing and medical students for hepatitis C and HIV. Aziz contends that the risks of transmission of blood borne diseases from health care workers to patients is very low. In fact, he suggests that more health care workers acquire blood borne pathogens from patients rather than the other way around. Aziz thinks the UK testing guidelines go against many UK laws, which are meant to protect people from discrimination and from invasions of privacy. He believes it is unethical and unfair to require health care workers to be tested for HIV or hepatitis C before they begin their careers. Aziz is a registered nurse and a senior lecturer in primary care at the University of Wolverhamptom in the UK.

For many years, there has been an understanding between healthcare workers and their patients in which no one would expect to know the HIV or hepatitis C status of anyone else.

SOURCE: Bashyr Aziz, "Testing Times," *Nursing Management,* vol. 14, October 2007. Copyright © 2007 Royal College of Nursing Publishing Company. Reproduced by permission.

Unwritten Compact

This unwritten compact served both parties well because to demand information about the blood borne virus (BBV) status of the members of either group would be to deny their basic right to privacy.

After all, why should nurses and doctors wish to know about their patients' BBV status except where such knowledge affects their treatment? And why should patients wish to know about their nurses' and doctors' infectivity, except where this allows them to choose their carers?

In general, the compact has worked well. There is not a single documented case of HIV transmission from healthcare worker to patient in the UK [United Kingdom], although there have been five documented cases of occupationally acquired HIV in healthcare workers [according to the UK Health Protection Agency].

A nurse attends a patient in a London hospital. The author argues that because there have been only fifteen documented cases of hepatitis C transmission from health care workers to patients in the United Kingdom, mandatory testing is not needed. **(Fiona Hanson/PA Photos/Landov)**

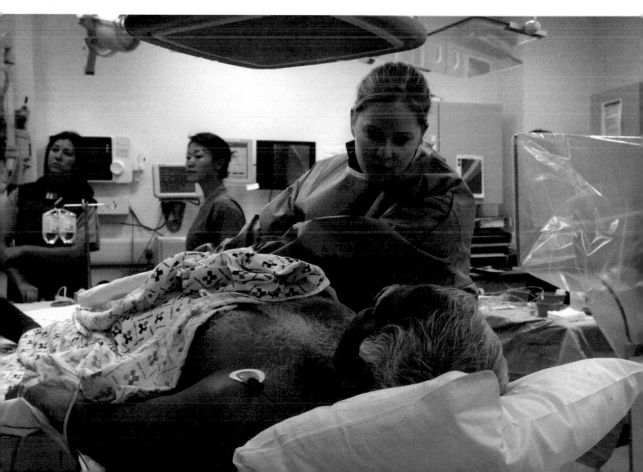

A further 14 probable cases of occupational acquisitions of HIV in healthcare workers have been diagnosed in the UK, but most of these involved people who had worked in countries of high HIV prevalence and so are presumed to have been infected outside the UK.

There have been five reported incidents in which healthcare workers have transmitted hepatitis C to 15 patients during invasive, or "exposure prone," procedures [according to the UK Department of Health (DH)].

The number of such transmissions in health care should not increase as long as medical, surgical, midwifery and dental practice requires that effective barriers and universal precautions are applied in all exposure prone procedures, on the assumption that every patient and every healthcare worker is a potential carrier of BBVs.

New Guidelines Are Suspect

In March 2007, however, the compact was broken when the DH issued guidelines that required all new applicants to nursing, midwifery or dentistry schools who expect to carry out exposure prone procedures to be tested once for HIV and hepatitis C.

In most areas of the UK, these guidelines should have been in place last month [September 2007], in time for the start of the new academic year. They seem to have been received by nursing and medical schools, as well as teaching hospitals, without a murmur of protest, the prevalent attitude apparently being that, if the DH wishes it, so be it.

They appear to require that aspirant nurses or midwives who are found to be carriers of HIV or hepatitis C are discouraged or even barred from following their chosen careers, and given advice on pursuing alternative careers.

This requirement is made without regard to the high probability that some current staff are HIV or hepatitis C positive and their removal will represent a significant loss of talent from the healthcare services.

They also represent a major infringement of people's rights under the [UK] Disability Discrimination Act 1995, the Human Rights Act 1998 and the Equality Act 2006.

A Violation of Disability Laws

The Disability Discrimination Act 1995 for example requires that applicants are not denied training or work due to long term medical conditions, which presumably include HIV and hepatitis C.

The argument made by some potential employers or school admission staff that, because the health and safety of patients take precedence over the right to privacy of healthcare workers, all new applicants should be tested can be met by the counter argument that, if this is so, all current doctors and nurses should be tested too.

Moreover, because the results of blood tests made now may not be the same as those made next year, or in five or ten years' time, such tests must be carried out regularly.

To carry out blood tests in this way would be totally impractical of course, not least because many healthcare workers may be found to be BBV carriers and would have to be redeployed into "safe" areas of practice.

> **FAST FACT**
>
> Studies indicate that African Americans are less likely to respond to hepatitis C combination treatment than are whites.

Of course, aspiring nurses and doctors could skip the tests if they give firm undertakings that they will not enter specialisms that require the carrying out of exposure prone procedures, just as students who undergo the tests and are found to be "BBV positive" will presumably be advised to do the same.

But in either case, it is unclear how many nursing or medical students can, at the start of their training, identify the areas in which they will work later.

Moreover, once nursing or medical students have been cleared by occupational health staff and have started

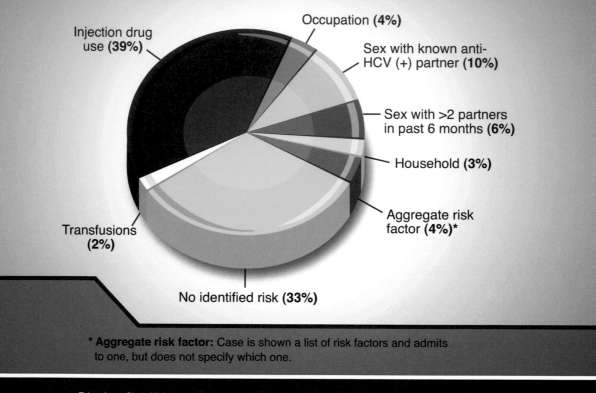

Risk Factors for Hepatitis C in the United States, 2001–2004

Injection drug use (39%)

Occupation (4%)

Sex with known anti-HCV (+) partner (10%)

Sex with >2 partners in past 6 months (6%)

Household (3%)

Aggregate risk factor (4%)*

Transfusions (2%)

No identified risk (33%)

* Aggregate risk factor: Case is shown a list of risk factors and admits to one, but does not specify which one.

Taken from: Cindy Weinbaum, "Issues for the Prevention and Control of HCV Infection in the United States," Division of Viral Hepatitis, Centers for Disease Control and Prevention, December 2008.

their training, they may be able to work in any exposure prone area of practice they choose, despite the stipulation of some schools and trusts that the tests should be carried out on all students who embark on careers for example in surgery.

It is difficult to see therefore how this stipulation can be enforced in cases of students who will be at the same level as the thousands of existing nursing and medical students who have not had to undergo tests.

PERSPECTIVES ON DISEASES AND DISORDERS

A Violation of Privacy Rights

Students found to be BBV positive will presumably be given clearance with restrictions such as: "This person is fit for training, but should not be involved in exposure prone work." They will not have bold red stamps saying, "Beware, this person is a BBV hazard!" on their clearance forms, but the effect on their careers will be the same as if they had.

This contravenes [is contrary to] the [UK] Data Protection Act 1998, which makes it clear that providing implicit information that allows a recipient of information to reach a conclusion about the data subject's personal information is unlawful regardless of whether the information is explicit, and what is more personal than one's HIV or hepatitis C status?

In addition, the Human Rights Act 1998 provides for a right to privacy.

When, in the process of seeking training for careers, people are informed that they are carriers of HIV or hepatitis C, they may have cause to be grateful because they can quickly seek treatment that may delay the onset of full blown illness.

But being informed in this way guarantees that their lives will never be the same again, especially when they seek life insurance, mortgages or even a "normal" family life, all of which are enshrined as human rights.

The compact between healthcare workers and patients has been effective for many years. Recently, the incidence of HIV and hepatitis C infection has increased but there is little evidence that this is caused by transmission from healthcare workers.

On the contrary, there is every sign that the government is failing to get across to people its "safe sex" and "safe drugs" messages.

Unfair and Unethical

By forcing aspirant healthcare workers to undergo tests for BBVs, the DH is signalling that healthcare workers who are carriers represent a risk to their patients, in which case it should start testing all healthcare workers who carry out exposure prone procedures and be prepared to deal with the consequences.

But, by not subjecting all patients who require exposure prone procedures to the same test, the DH is also suggesting that it cares more about the safety of its patients than it does about that of its own workforce.

Of course, it would be unfair and unethical for patients to be denied care simply because they are BBV carriers; but it is also unfair and unethical for people to be denied the right to become healthcare workers in areas of their choosing for the same reason.

By issuing these guidelines, the DH has opened a hornet's nest, the implications of which may be the denial for many of potential careers in health care.

The Hepatitis B Vaccine Causes Multiple Sclerosis

David Kirby

In the following viewpoint David Kirby asserts that the hepatitis B vaccine causes multiple sclerosis (MS) and other diseases. According to Kirby, the U.S. court designated by law to handle vaccine injury claims—referred to as the Vaccine Court—has issued several rulings that indicate that the hepatitis B vaccine may be responsible for causing MS and other demyelinating diseases. In MS, the myelin sheath which surrounds nerve cells is slowly destroyed. Expert witnesses in one case before the Vaccine Court testified that the hepatitis B vaccine may cause the body's own immune system to attack myelin. Kirby ponders whether these Vaccine Court rulings make it more likely that the court will find that there is an association between autism and thimerosal, the mercury-based preservative in the measles, mumps, and rubella vaccine. Kirby is the author of the book *Evidence of Harm: Mercury in Vaccines and the Autism Epidemic; A Medical Controversy*. He has written for several national magazines and is a blogger for the *Huffington Post* and the *Age of Autism*.

SOURCE: David Kirby, "Vaccine Court: Hepatitis B Shot Caused MS," AgeofAutism.com, February 3, 2009. Reproduced by permission.

All eyes are on Vaccine Court this week [in February 2009], as people await rulings in the autism "test cases" on MMR [measles, mumps, and rubella vaccine] and thimerosal. But another omnibus [covering many things] proceeding involving Hepatitis B vaccine and autoimmune disorders in adults, including MS [multiple sclerosis], has already been quietly ruling in favor of several petitioners.

The most recent case was announced about a week ago. In it, the Court ruled that the victim, an adult female, had contracted a form of demyelinating disease and MS, and eventually died, after receiving the Hepatitis B vaccine series. It was just the most recent case in a rash of rulings in the omnibus proceeding dealing with hepatitis B vaccine and "demyelinating diseases such as transverse myelitis (TM), Guillain-Barré syndrome (GBS), chronic inflammatory demyelinating disease (CIDP), and multiple sclerosis (MS)," according to court papers.

Injury from Hepatitis B Vaccine

"Petitioner has prevailed on the issue of entitlement. The medical records during decedent's final hospitalization reflect that she died from demyelinating disease. Not only did decedent have a vaccine injury, but also her death was vaccine-related," wrote the Special Master in the case.

Interestingly, the US government chose not to present any expert witnesses, nor to contest the case any further.

But the family of the deceased woman had presented testimony from an expert witness who stated that, "It is biologically plausible for hepatitis B to cause demyelination because vaccines are composed of organic compounds of viral or bacterial origin, whether recombinant or otherwise, whose purpose is to initiate an immune response in the recipient," the Court noted in the ruling. "But if any of the vaccine antigens shares a homology with the recipient's antigens, the host's immune response will attack both the vaccine antigens and the host's antigens, resulting in an autoimmune response. This concept is also known as molecular mimicry and is well-established in immunology."

In the last few years, it turns out, the Federal Vaccine Court has issued a number of rulings in favor of petitioners seeking compensation for Hepatitis B vaccine–related demyelinating diseases, especially MS.

Disagreeing with the IOM

What is also notable about all the Hep B rulings is that they fly in the face of the reasoned opinion of an IOM [Institute of Medicine] panel that looked into the matter in 2002. That committee determined that "the epidemiological evidence favors rejection of a causal relationship between the hepatitis B vaccine in adults and multiple sclerosis." Likewise, the panel said that it "does not recommend that national and federal vaccine advisory bodies review the hepatitis B vaccine on the basis of concerns about demyelinating disorders."

Apparently, Vaccine Court Special Masters are willing to make their rulings independent of what the IOM has decreed (and given the IOM's spotty track record on the etiology [causes or origins] of illnesses such as Agent Orange and Gulf War Syndrome, perhaps there is a solid legal underpinning for that).

So, what does any of this have to do with the autism cases? Perhaps nothing. But, if the autism Special Masters suggest that more research is needed, one area that scientists may want to explore is demyelination in autism and its many potential causes.

> **FAST FACT**
>
> According to the 2007 National Immunization Survey, 87.6 percent of American teens aged thirteen through seventeen had received the complete series of the hepatitis B vaccine.

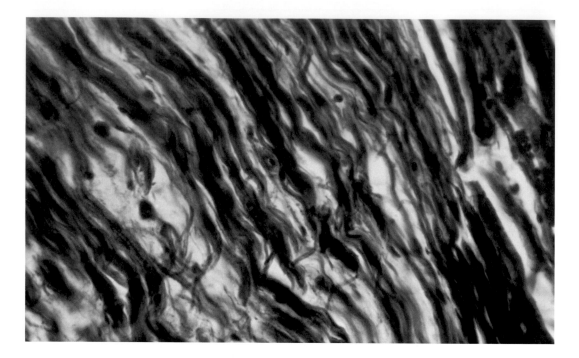

A light micrograph shows the effects of demyelination on nerve fibers. The black area indicates the loss of myelin, which causes disruption of electrical signals to the nerves. Hepatitis B vaccine is suspected as the cause. (CNRI/Photo Researchers, Inc.)

Vaccine-Myelin Association

Myelin is the fatty acid sheath that protects and insulates nerve cells and the brain. Some people with autoimmune disorders, including MS, present with damage to myelin in the brain.

Myelin damage has long been suspected in autism, though the jury is still out on this question. One thing that does seem to be certain is that children with ASD [autism spectrum disorder] appear to have unusually high levels of antibodies to myelin basic protein, or MBP. That would suggest they might have myelin damage as well. Some studies have also shown highly elevated levels (up to 90%) of MBP antibodies in ASD children who received the MMR vaccine. The development of MBP antibodies could possibly be caused by a reaction to the live measles virus in the vaccine, because the virus may mimic the molecular structure of MBP. (The finding of antibodies to MBP is also associated with MS, which is a demyelinating disorder.)

This vaccine-myelin association was also supported by a study in the October, 2008 issue of the journal *Neurology*. It reported that exposure to Hep B vaccine in children was associated with a 50% increased risk for CNS [central nervous system] inflammatory demyelination of 50 percent. This was especially true for children who got GlaxoSmithKline's Engerix B vaccine, in which case

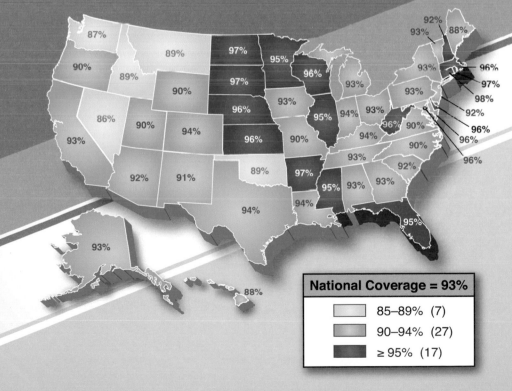

Hepatitis B Vaccination Coverage of Children Aged Nineteen Months to Thirty-five Months

In most states, 90 percent of children nineteen months to thirty-five months of age had received three or more doses of the hepatitis B vaccine (July 2007–June 2008).

National Coverage = 93%	
	85–89% (7)
	90–94% (27)
	≥ 95% (17)

Taken from: Centers for Disease Control and Prevention.

the risk was elevated by 74%. Among ASD children with confirmed multiple sclerosis, the risk increased by 177%.

"Hepatitis B vaccination does not generally increase the risk of CNS inflammatory demyelination in childhood," the authors concluded. "However, the Engerix B vaccine appears to increase this risk, particularly for confirmed multiple sclerosis, in the longer term. Our results require confirmation in future studies."

Of course more studies are needed, but it is becoming more difficult these days to argue that there is no active immune/inflammatory response going on in the brains of autistic individuals, and even harder to contest that MBP is associated with at least one aspect of that response, although there are likely others. The MBP findings are not 100% concordant [harmonious], but there is a fair amount of supportive evidence. . . .

If the HepB series can destroy myelin in some kids and adults, and cause full-blown MS in adults, then is it really that "fringe" to investigate the plausibility of a biological mechanism whereby some vaccines (including MMR) in a subset of susceptible infants might produce symptoms that are characteristic of autism and/or other neuro-developmental disorders?

For years, the US Government and the IOM have insisted that Hepatitis B vaccine does not and can not cause MS. But the Federal Vaccine Court has now, essentially, overturned that opinion. Will the Court now do the same for vaccines and autism? I don't think so—not this week. But it just might keep that door slightly ajar for the future.

The Hepatitis B Vaccine Does Not Cause Multiple Sclerosis

Immunization Safety Office: Centers for Disease Control and Prevention

In the following viewpoint the Immunization Safety Office at the Centers for Disease Control and Prevention (CDC) says no proof supports the notion that the hepatitis B vaccine causes multiple sclerosis (MS). The CDC points to the results of several research studies that show no association between MS and the vaccine. The agency says it will continue to monitor and review the safety of the hepatitis B vaccine. However, Americans have no reason to delay or avoid getting the vaccine. The CDC is the lead federal agency responsible for the control of infectious and chronic diseases. The agency's Immunization Safety Office identifies possible vaccine side effects and conducts studies to determine whether a health problem is caused by a specific vaccine.

Numerous studies have evaluated a possible relationship between hepatitis B vaccination and multiple sclerosis (MS). The weight of the

SOURCE: "Hepatitis B Vaccine and Concerns About Multiple Sclerosis (MS)," CDC.gov, October 14, 2008. Information obtained from the Centers for Disease Control and Prevention. www.cdc.gov.

available scientific evidence does not support the suggestion that hepatitis B vaccine causes or worsens MS.
. . .

MS Is a Central Nervous System Disease

Multiple Sclerosis (MS) is a disease of the central nervous system characterized by the destruction of the myelin sheath surrounding neurons, resulting in the formation of "plaques." Because they involve the destruction of the myelin sheath that covers nerve tissue, diseases such as MS are known as "demyelinating" diseases.

MS is a progressive and usually fluctuating disease with exacerbations (patients feeling worse) and remissions (patients feeling better) over many decades. In many patients with MS, permanent disability and even death can occur. The cause of MS is unknown. The most widely held hypothesis is that MS occurs in patients with a genetic susceptibility and is "triggered" by certain environmental factors.

MS is 3 times more common in women than men, with diagnosis usually made as young adults; however, it has been estimated that between 2 to 5% of cases begin before age 16. Since MS is not widely recognized as a childhood disorder, diagnosis is often missed or delayed. In addition, many of its symptoms are similar to those of other pediatric neurological conditions, leukodystrophies and metabolic disorders. Diagnosis in childhood is difficult due to the lack of universally accepted diagnostic criteria.

Research Shows No Link Between Hepatitis B Vaccine and MS

Most published scientific studies do not support a causal relationship between hepatitis B vaccination and MS or other demyelinating diseases. Examples of this scientific evidence are as follows:

Extensive pre-licensure clinical trials did not document such an effect.

Hundreds of millions of people worldwide have received hepatitis B vaccine without developing MS (or any other autoimmune disease). This finding provides important evidence as well as an appropriate framework for assessing this possible association—namely, that if vaccination causes MS, it does so extremely rarely.

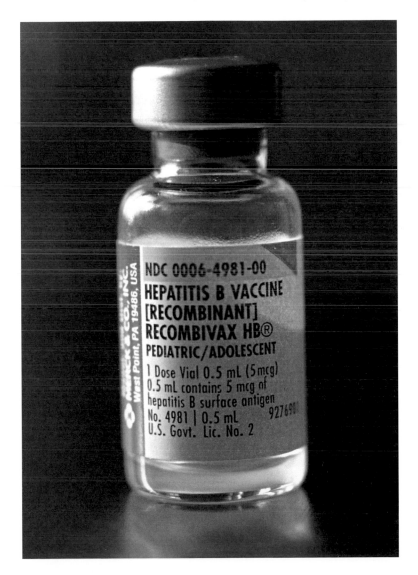

The viewpoint author cites several studies indicating that there is no direct link between hepatitis B vaccine and multiple sclerosis. (Michelle Del Guercio/ Photo Researchers, Inc.)

Due to the large number of vaccinations administered worldwide, surveillance systems in the United States, France, and elsewhere expect to receive reports of MS that are only temporally (by chance alone) associated with vaccines.

According to a study published in the Oct. 8, 2000, online issue of *Neurology*, the majority of children vaccinated against hepatitis B are not at an increased risk of developing CNS [central nervous system] inflammatory demyelination. 349 children with a first episode of acute CNS inflammatory demyelination before age 16 were matched to 2,941 healthy controls and evaluated for use of hepatitis B vaccination. When subjects were restricted to those compliant with vaccination, children who received a specific type of hepatitis B vaccine (Engerix B) more than 3 years earlier were found to have a slightly increased risk of developing an acute CNS demyelinating event and a slightly higher risk of having a confirmed diagnosis of MS. The findings in this paper cannot be taken as confirmation that the vaccine caused MS. Further studies are needed to confirm this observation, and then, if confirmed, to determine whether this is a causal relationship.

A study conducted in France from 1994 to 2003 did not find a relationship between vaccination for hepatitis B and the development of childhood-onset multiple sclerosis. The 143 cases included children with onset of MS before [the] age of 16 years. 1,122 control subjects were selected randomly from the general French population. The rate of a first episode of MS was not increased for hepatitis B vaccination.

A study was conducted using Vaccine Safety Datalink (VSD) project to assess the association between hepatitis B vaccination and demyelinating diseases such as MS among members of 3 large managed care organizations (MCOs) on the west coast of the United States. The study included 422 adult cases (people with demyelinating dis-

FAST FACT

According to the Autism Society of America, 1 million to 2.5 million Americans have autism.

ease) and 921 matched controls (people of similar age, gender, and MCO status who did not have demyelinating disease). The researchers concluded that hepatitis B vaccination was not associated with demyelinating disease in the study population.

[A.] Ascherio and colleagues evaluated the possible association between hepatitis B vaccination and MS. The study included 192 women with MS and 645 controls. The authors concluded that there was no association between hepatitis B vaccination and MS.

A study was conducted in Europe to evaluate whether MS relapses were associated with receipt of hepatitis B, tetanus, or influenza vaccines. The study included 643 individuals with relapsing MS. The researchers concluded that there was no evidence of an association between recent receipt of hepatitis B vaccine (or tetanus or influenza vaccination) and MS relapses.

[A.D.] Sadovnick and [D.W.] Scheifele investigated multiple sclerosis in 578,308 adolescents in British Columbia before and after hepatitis B vaccination programs were implemented. The authors found no evidence of a link between hepatitis B vaccination and multiple sclerosis or other demyelinating disease.

An analysis of a U.S. pharmacy benefits management database did not find a statistically significant association between claims for hepatitis B vaccination and subsequent claims for treatment of CNS demyelinating disorders. . . .

Expert Review

CDC and the National Institutes of Health (NIH) asked the National Academy of Sciences, Institute of Medicine [IOM] to establish an independent expert committee to review hypotheses about existing and emerging immunization safety concerns. The review will involve an assessment of factors such as the biologic mechanisms of the hypothesis, competing alternative hypotheses, as well as the available scientific evidence to date.

In 2002, the IOM reviewed the evidence of a possible causal association between hepatitis B vaccine and demyelinating neurological disorders, including MS in adults. The committee found that the epidemiological evidence does not support a causal relationship between hepatitis B vaccine in adults and multiple sclerosis. . . .

Vaccination for Hepatitis B Should Not Be Delayed

Results from studies that have examined the possible association between hepatitis B vaccination and MS are

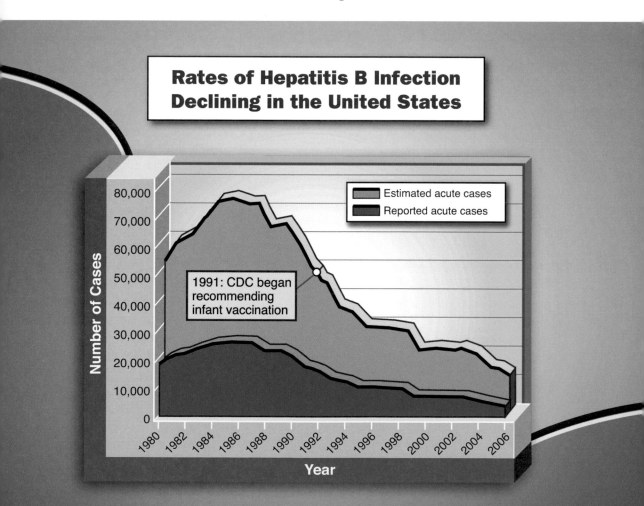

Rates of Hepatitis B Infection Declining in the United States

1991: CDC began recommending infant vaccination

Taken from: "FAQs for Health Professionals," Centers of Disease Control and Prevention, Division of Viral Hepatitis, updated January 27, 2009.

reassuring and support current recommendations for immunizing against hepatitis B. Concern regarding the alleged association between hepatitis B vaccination and MS must be weighed against the vaccine's ability to prevent risks associated with hepatitis B virus infection.

CDC Continues to Monitor Vaccine Safety

CDC takes concerns about vaccines and immune system diseases and disorders very seriously. Researchers at CDC and elsewhere have conducted studies to examine the possible link between vaccines and autoimmune conditions like MS, diabetes, and asthma. These studies have been reassuring, providing no evidence to suggest a link between vaccines and autoimmune conditions.

As part of ongoing vaccine safety surveillance, CDC will continue to conduct research to examine the effects vaccines may have on the immune system.

Chimpanzees Are Needed for Research on Hepatitis and Other Diseases

Foundation for Biomedical Research

In the following viewpoint the Foundation for Biomedical Research (FBR) contends that nonhuman primates, such as chimpanzees and monkeys, are needed for many different kinds of biomedical research. According to the FBR, scientists use chimpanzees in hepatitis B and C research because they are susceptible to these diseases in the same way that humans are. The foundation says that chimpanzee research has contributed to the development of the hepatitis B vaccine and helped to eliminate the incidence of this disease. The FBR argues that nonhuman primates are essential for biomedical research because of their close relationship to humans. The Foundation for Biomedical Research is a nonprofit organization supporting humane and responsible animal research.

L ess than ¼ of one percent of all lab animals used in the U.S. are non-human primates. Approximately 30 different species are studied by the research community. Many historic scientific breakthroughs, such as the discovery of the Rh factor and the development of

SOURCE: "Non-Human Primates: The Essential Need for Animals in Medical Research," fbresearch.org, 2001. Reproduced by permission.

a live polio virus vaccine were achieved through research with non-human primates. Today they are considered extremely important models in many areas of medicine because of their close relationship to humans.

AIDS—Acquired Immune Deficiency Syndrome

Scientists face major challenges in their quest to develop a vaccine for human immunodeficiency virus (HIV), the agent that causes AIDS. Having no human model of protection to guide them, medical researchers depend heavily on monkeys for the development of promising strategies to protect people from this disease. Vaccines containing various strains of a simian [related to apes or monkeys] immunodeficiency virus (SIV), a closely related virus that follows a disease course similar to HIV, or a hybrid [simian/human] immunodeficiency virus (SHIV) are being tested in macaque monkeys, and several research groups have successfully vaccinated monkeys with viral preparations that reduce viral load and halt disease progression. If these results can be generalized to humans, the vaccines may be used to treat HIV-infected persons.

Hepatitis B and C

Chimpanzees are uniquely susceptible to human hepatitis virus infections and serve as an important study model for this global public health problem. Research with chimpanzees has virtually eradicated hepatitis B and C infections acquired through blood transfusions, a landmark achievement in the control of viral hepatitis. Commercially available hepatitis B vaccines have prevented the development of cirrhosis and liver cancer in millions of people. Because no vaccine for hepatitis C infections is yet available, scientists continue to study the pathogenesis [development] of this disease in chimpanzees to gain a better understanding of the infection process, to improve current treatment modalities, and to pave the way for the development of an effective vaccine.

The author says chimpanzees are vital to hepatitis research because studies of the primates have helped eradicate the transmission of hepatitis B and C through blood transfusions. **(Lawrence Migdale/ Photo Researchers, Inc.)**

Malaria

Researchers are beginning to overcome some of the enormous obstacles in developing a vaccine against malaria, a disease that affects millions of people annually. New world monkeys and chimpanzees are the only species suitable for vaccine evaluation because they are susceptible to the same strains of the parasites that cause human malaria. Unlike simpler organisms, the malaria parasite has many chromosomes, thousands of genes, and a four-stage life cycle as it passes from mosquitoes to humans and back again. A number of promising vaccines that attack the organism at every vulnerable point in its life cycle are being tested. Some of these have successfully stimulated protective responses in animals and may soon be ready for human trials.

Acute Respiratory Disease

Respiratory syncytial virus (RSV) can cause life-threatening respiratory infections in infants, young children and the elderly. Since there is no effective therapy, an RSV vaccine is a high medical priority in the U.S. Researchers are designing vaccines containing live, weakened viruses that are suitable for applying with nose drops. These vaccines are being tested for their ability to protect chimpanzees,

"Honey, can you believe we share 99% of our DNA with chimps?" Cartoon by Wilbur Dawbarn. www.Cartoonstock.com.

the only animal that is naturally infected by RSV and develops an illness with symptoms similar to those seen in humans.

Periodontal Disease

Microbial infection of the tissue supporting teeth is the most common cause of bone and tooth loss in humans and may be an important risk factor for cardiovascular disease. Periodontitis is also a health problem for captive primates, making these species excellent models for studying the connection between chronic oral infections and systemic disease. Several groups of researchers have shown that immunizing monkeys with a vaccine containing a killed oral bacterium can halt infection and suppress bone loss.

FAST FACT

According to the World Health Organization, the hepatitis B virus is fifty to one hundred times more infectious than HIV.

Aging and Nutrition

Scientists are currently studying the effects of long-term calorie restriction (CR) on the biology of aging in macaque monkeys. They have learned that a reduction in calories over a period of several years lowers body temperature, slows metabolism, lessens the risk of cardiovascular disease, and reduces predisposition toward diabetes. Long-term studies of CR have increased the life span of monkeys.

Brain Biology

Because they share many features of brain biology and structure with humans, non-human primates are extremely valuable models for studying normal brain function and brain-related diseases, including mental, neurological, and addictive disorders. Many of the functional regions of the cerebral cortex that are present and identifiable in monkeys and other small primates have provided a precise map of the brain circuitry involved in visual and auditory perception, learning and memory deficits, and brain and spinal cord injuries.

Alzheimer's Disease

The decline of memory and other mental functions in patients with Alzheimer's disease (AD) is associated with the loss of or damage to cholinergic nerve cells that use the chemical acetylcholine to transmit messages to other cells in the brain. Age-related reduction in the functions of these nerve cells also occurs in primate species. Scientists have shown that grafting genetically modified cells to produce nerve growth factor (NGF) directly into the brains of macaque monkeys is a safe procedure that enhances the survival and function of the cholinergic nerve cells. Such studies are now being extended to humans in an attempt to slow the loss of memory in patients with AD.

Parkinson's Disease

Parkinson's disease (PD) is a slow, progressive disease, generally found in the aged, that is characterized by tremors. Scientists know that the disease is associated with degeneration of brain cells that produce a chemical (neurotransmitter) called dopamine. Recently, they found a new method to deliver the gene that produces GLNF (a factor that protects brain cells) directly into the brains of monkeys. The treatment successfully prevented the progression and reversed the symptoms of PD. Clinical testing to forestall human disease is under consideration.

Chimpanzees Should Not Be Used for Hepatitis Research

Theodora Capaldo and Jarrod Bailey

In the following viewpoint Theodora Capaldo and Jarrod Bailey contend that chimpanzees should not be used for hepatitis B and C research, pointing out that researchers have other options that do not require the use of chimpanzees. The authors refute the claim that chimpanzees were critical for many important discoveries, such as the hepatitis B vaccine. Chimpanzees' only use in this discovery, according to Capaldo and Bailey, was to serve as "living test tubes" in which to grow the virus. Chimpanzees used for research endure grueling and painful procedures—repeatedly—and suffer from long-term trauma. Hepatitis research, the authors argue, can and should proceed without the use of chimpanzees. Capaldo is president of the New England Anti-Vivisection Society and coordinator of Project R&R (Release & Restitution for Chimpanzees in U.S. Laboratories). Bailey, who has published numerous papers on non-animal research methods, is the science advisor for Project R & R.

Chimpanzees are most widely used in hepatitis C research but are also used for hepatitis A and B research. In 2006, the National Institutes of Health (NIH) spent approximately $11 million on infectious disease research. Of that amount, roughly 65% was for hepatitis C research alone.

Hepatitis research on chimpanzees continues despite arguments challenging its scientific worth. As with the HIV virus, chimpanzees respond differently to being infected with the hepatitis C virus (HCV) compared to humans.

After years of research on chimpanzees costing millions of taxpayer dollars, there is still no definitive cure. However, human-centered research, such as in vitro studies involving human cell cultures, is showing promising results and should therefore be pursued more aggressively on account of its greater human relevance.

About Hepatitis

Hepatitis is characterized by inflammation of the liver that can be acute and self-limiting, or chronic, degenerative, and fatal. It has a variety of causes including drug and alcohol abuse, drug toxicity, and a range of viral pathogens, the most common of which are known as hepatitis A, B, or C. Typical symptoms are jaundice, fever, and liver enlargement.

Although hepatitis B (HBV) is the most prevalent of the three, the hepatitis C virus (HCV) is [in humans] "responsible for 40% of chronic liver disease in the U.S." and "is a leading cause of liver failure and transplants." Worldwide, nearly 200 million people are affected by HCV. Unlike hepatitis C, hepatitis A does not lead to chronic liver infections, while hepatitis B can range from a short-term illness to a chronic one resulting in liver cancer.

Limitations in Using Chimpanzees for Hepatitis C Research

Differences between HCV infections in humans vs. chimpanzees:

- The likelihood of human HCV infections becoming chronic is 75–85%; the likelihood for chimpanzees is only 30–50%.
- Humans with HCV often develop cirrhosis of the liver, a chronic degenerative condition. Chimpanzees do not.
- Humans with HCV frequently develop liver cancer; chimpanzees rarely do.
- In humans, the virus can be transferred from the mother to the fetus; this does not occur in chimpanzees.

Similar to the issues with HIV chimpanzee research, these differences call into question whether or not it is likely that a vaccine for human HCV will be developed using chimpanzees—arguably, the scale of the biological differences between humans and chimpanzees underlying these observations means that chimpanzees cannot serve as a reliable and predictive model.

While studying the differences between humans and other species can inform science, it can (and has) led researchers to erroneous conclusions or dead ends. Despite its limitations, well over $7 million in NIH funding was spent on HCV research involving chimpanzees in 2006.

In July 2005, hepatitis C researchers reported a breakthrough in the technology to grow the virus entirely in cell culture. Increased funding should be channeled into human clinical studies and *in vitro* [outside a living organism] methods of growing infectious agents for research.

FAST FACT

According to the American Anti-vivisection Society, 62,315 nonhuman primates were used for research in 2006, up from 42,298 in 1973.

The creation of a tissue culture of HCV infected human cells is important because it provides a model of the virus replicating in its "natural environment" and therefore creates a relevant system for the study of HCV pathology, and the testing of potential treatments and vaccines, in a human context.

Chimpanzees Are Not Essential for Hepatitis B Research

As with HCV infection, the physiology of the chimpanzees' response differs markedly from human infection. Essentially, a chimpanzee infected with HBV will not become sick, while humans exhibit traditional symptoms of liver disease.

Differences between HBV infections in humans vs. chimpanzees:

- Chimpanzees are essentially asymptomatic when infected; humans are not.
- Chimpanzees continue to produce the virus as long as it is in their body; humans do not.
- The liver, which is the organ primarily affected, is not affected in chimpanzees as it is in humans.
- Liver enzymes, which are measured to assess the progression of the disease, respond differently in humans and chimpanzees.

Scientists commonly cite the development of the hepatitis B vaccine as an example of the essential role of chimpanzees in infectious disease research. However, the development of the hepatitis B vaccine amounted to little more than using chimpanzee bodies as "test tubes" to grow the virus—a method that has been replaced with in vitro methods. It did not come about through studying the physiology of the disease in their bodies. In actuality the first hepatitis B vaccine was made from the blood of infected humans, and vaccines are now made using genetically engineered yeast.

Number of Hepatitis-Infected Chimpanzees

According to a 1997 report funded by NIH, "195 animals . . . participated in hepatitis virus research" at six research facilities. The report also noted, "That number substantially underestimates the total used, because of normal attrition and the fact that many chimpanzees housed at New York University's Laboratory of Experimental Medicine and Surgery in Primates (LEMSIP) were not counted but are known to have been used in HBV studies."

Given the prevalence of hepatitis research currently funded by NIH—35 in 2008—an accurate number for hepatitis infected chimpanzees is unknown.

At the Southwest National Primate Research Center (SNPRC), their 166 chimpanzees are used in HBV, HCV, and/or HIV research. In addition to using chimpanzees as a model for HCV infection, chimpanzee studies within Southwest's HCV program include:

> studies on the basis of protective immunity and analysis of HCV induced changes in liver gene expression by DNA microarray technology. . . . In addition, the program performs research in collaboration with a number of pharmaceutical companies, mostly for the testing of HCV antivirals in chimpanzees.

What Happens to Chimpanzees During Hepatitis Research

Hepatitis studies can be painful and grueling for chimpanzees. In addition to being isolated in sterile biocontainment facilities, the chimpanzees are subjected to frequent serial blood draws, other inoculations, and liver biopsies.

Liver biopsies are done using anesthesia and therefore require prior immobilization of the chimpanzee with

a chemical agent (usually Ketamine). Lab technicians typically administer the drug to chimpanzees through a process known as "a knockdown" in which pre-loaded syringes are fired through a dart gun.

It is not unusual for a chimpanzee to be surrounded by laboratory personnel in order to be subdued or for the chimpanzee to be shot in vulnerable parts of their body—while thrashing about futilely trying to avoid the dart gun—such as their eye or genitals, or even puncturing and collapsing a lung. (Some chimpanzees have been trained to accept injections.)

Chimpanzees traumatized by serving as hepatitis research subjects may end up living in sanctuaries like this one in Florida. The sanctuary houses over three-hundred chimps rescued from medical labs. (**Robert Gallagher/Aurora/Getty Images**)

Chimpanzees who have lived through these ordeals and are now in sanctuaries are living testimony to the long-term trauma such procedures cause. Fauna Foundation in Quebec is currently home to 13 chimpanzees nearly all of whom have come out of labs. Extensive and detailed medical histories offer a window into their lives. Consider the story of Billy Jo (now deceased) as recounted by Fauna:

> In 14 years at the lab, Ch-447, Billy Jo was knocked down over 289 times—65 by dart with 4 or 5 men surrounding his cage pummeling darts into his body to anaesthetize him for a routine blood draw. In the lab he would shake his cage back and forth trying desperately to prevent anyone from approaching. Till the end of his life, Billy could not bear to have strangers grouped in front of him.
>
> In addition to several HIV challenges, Billy endured some 40 punch liver biopsies, 3 open wedge liver biopsies, 3 bone marrow biopsies and 2 lymph node biopsies with no tangible or practical results. He also chewed off his thumbs waking up alone from knockdowns when no one was around to care for him. During one fit of anxiety, he bit off his index finger. Anxious, aggressive, and fearful, Billy banged incessantly on his cage, rocking and staring into space when left alone. Even in sanctuary, Billy was plagued by anxiety attacks—attacks so bad that they left this majestic adult male chimpanzee choking, gagging and convulsing. . . .

Hepatitis Research Without Chimpanzees

It is claimed that chimpanzees are the only nonhuman animal capable of being infected with the virus for hepatitis C and other strains. While this may be true, it does not follow that the only way to pursue research into treatment for hepatitis is by infecting chimpanzees or

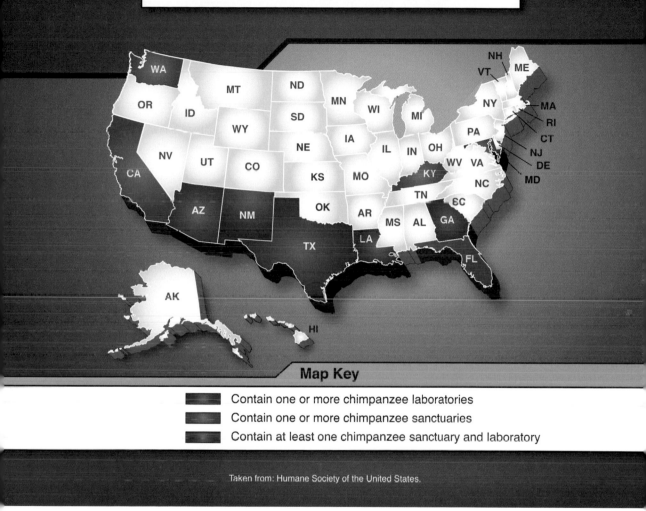

Chimpanzee Research Facilities and Sanctuaries in the United States

Map Key

■ Contain one or more chimpanzee laboratories
■ Contain one or more chimpanzee sanctuaries
■ Contain at least one chimpanzee sanctuary and laboratory

Taken from: Humane Society of the United States.

that such research may lead to a cure (chimpanzees are also the only species who can be infected with the HIV virus, a point that proved irrelevant to their usefulness in HIV research).

Much hepatitis research today is carried out through observation and clinical trials on humans with hepatitis. Observation and analysis of a patient's condition is, and always has been, a central component of medical research.

Examining the number of NIH funded projects for human clinical studies versus chimpanzee studies on hepatitis suggests that chimpanzees studies represent a small percentage of total studies. In 2008, NIH funded 220 human hepatitis trials and only 35 research projects involving the use of chimpanzees.

The millions of dollars spent on the inefficient and ineffective use of chimpanzees as "test tubes" should be channeled into developing efficient and ethical means of culturing the virus.

CHAPTER 3

Personal Stories About Hepatitis

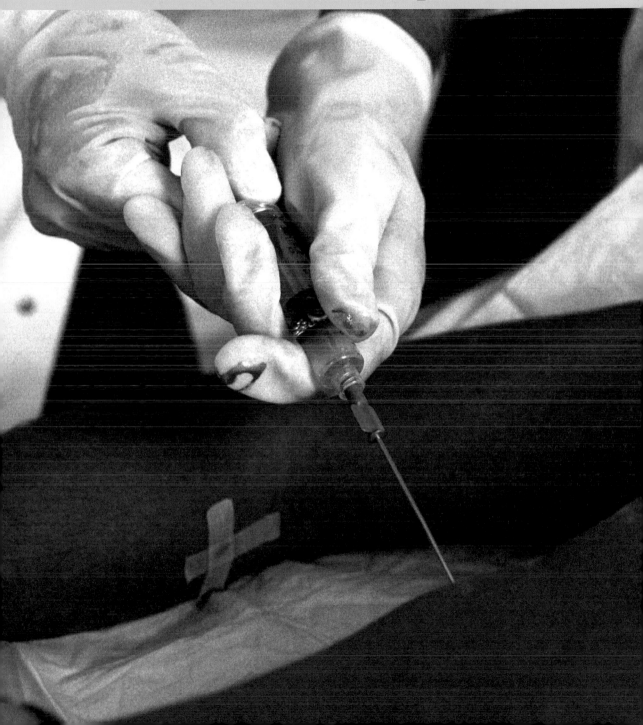

A Musician
Battles Hepatitis

David Crosby, interviewed by the *New York Post*

In the following article, the *New York Post* interviews musician David Crosby on his battle with hepatitis C. The contemporary musician of Crosby, Stills, Nash & Young shares his knowledge of the disease and gives thanks for the liver transplant that saved his life. Crosby informs the *New York Post* that within the United States there are close to 5 million cases of hepatitis and nearly 120 million worldwide. The *New York Post* is one of the nation's oldest daily newspapers.

D avid Crosby should probably be dead now, but this much-loved musician is still very much part of contemporary music, thanks to a donor liver he got seven years ago to replace his own, which was ravaged by the incurable disease hepatitis C. Crosby was hardly an angel during the '60s, '70s, and '80s.

He'd be the first to admit he ate a pharmacy of recreational drugs while writing some of the most memorable

Photo on previous page. A patient has a sample of liver tissue removed. The tissue will be tested for the presence of hepatitis. (Phanie/ Photo Researchers, Inc.)

music of his generation. But in the past seven years, he's been straight and sober, living life to it fullest. Family has become more important to him. The singer is the patriarch of a clan that includes two sons with his wife, Jan; a daughter who is 26; a 37-year-old son named James Raymond (Crosby knew nothing about him until 1994); a granddaughter; and Bailey and Beckett, his much-publicized genetic children with (musician) Melissa Etheridge and Julie Cypher. Crosby says donating his DNA to Etheridge and Cypher was an easy decision, although it earned him the title of Sperminator with late-night talk-show hosts.

Musician David Crosby, who had suffered from hepatitis C, was the fortunate recipient of a life-saving liver transplant. (AP Images)

Despite the ribbing he took, Crosby told *Rolling Stone* a couple of years ago that he was happy to oblige because "Melissa and Julie are good people, nice set of values, they're funnier than s - - - , and they got courage. All rare stuff."

Speaking from rehearsals for the Crosby Stills Nash & Young tour that lands at the Madison Square Garden for sold-out shows . . . [in February 2002], the avuncular music icon was robust and full of life.

Post: How are you feeling?

Crosby: Great. Very healthy. I have seven extra years on my life after I was supposed to be dead.

Post: You had a liver transplant, and you have hepatitis C.

Crosby: Yeah. It's a slow-moving disease, and it'll take another 20 years for it to kill this liver. I'll take the 20 years. Hep C is one of the worst problems the world has to face. Do you know the numbers?

Post: No.

Crosby: The World Health Organization says there are close to 5 million cases inside the United States right now, and worldwide they say there are 120 million. There is no cure for it, and we are merrily passing it along any time there's blood-to-blood contact. It's spreading very fast, and there are people out there who believe this is going to be worse than AIDS.

Post: Why?

Crosby: More cases, more people, more dead.

Post: Besides finding a cure, what should be done?

Crosby: People should get over the fear of going to the grave with all their parts, as if it mattered. It's nonsense. When the spirit is gone, it's ashes to ashes, dust to dust. After the spirit is gone, all that's left is parts that can save somebody else's life or their sight. Anybody who would take their body parts to the grave rather than help another human live is extremely weird, but they do.

Post: Your driver's license says you're an organ donor?

Crosby: No. I can't. I've got hep C. My parts are no good.

Post: Your voice is still pretty good. What can you say about the new tour?

Crosby: It was good last time around. This time, it's better. We really lucked out. We have a better band, there's absolutely no poison in the water and we're all being extremely nice to one another. And the music is so strong, it's ludicrous. We're gonna knock everyone's socks off.

Post: Why do you think Neil (Young) wanted to get back on the road?

Crosby: The last tour was fun for him. He liked it. He was also very affected by the terrorist attacks in the fall [September 11, 2001]. He told me that music has a healing quality, and I think he wanted to reach out to people.

Post: What are the tunes this time around that really stand out?

Crosby: Well, there's a number of songs that we didn't do last time out that are really working well. We've taken "Wooden Ships" to another level. "Deja Vu" is also just amazing.

Post: Anything new?

Crosby: Neil's song about Flight 93, "Let's Roll," is pretty excellent, very strong stuff. Things are coming along really well, but the band makes it easy.

Post: You mean Neil, Graham (Nash) and Stephen (Stills)?

Crosby: Yeah, but I'm talking about Booker T. and the MG's. We have Booker T. on organ, Duck Dunn on bass and Steve Potts on drums. The band locks us all together this time around.

Post: Who could have predicted 25 years ago that CSN&Y would be welded together with Booker T. and the MG's?

Crosby: It's a wild combo, but it works like a bandit.

> ## FAST FACT
>
> Studies show that almost one-third of alcoholics with liver disease are infected with hepatitis C.

An Officer with Hepatitis C Waits for a Liver Transplant

Hattie Brown Garrow

In the following article Hattie Brown Garrow tells the story of police officer Kurt Beach, his fight against hepatitis C, and his search for a living liver donor. Beach was a young rookie police officer when he contracted hepatitis C, providing unprotected CPR to a young child suffering from the birth defect spina bifida. According to Garrow, there were two casualties that night: The child did not make it, and Beach acquired an insidious virus. The author discusses how some twenty years later, the disease has taken a terrible toll on Beach. Yet, Beach has not given up. He hopes to find a new liver—from a living donor—and he hopes to return to the police force someday. Garrow is a reporter for the Virginian-Pilot.

K urt Beach, a rookie with the Smithfield Police Department, was the only officer working the midnight shift in February 1988 when a residential call came in. A child had stopped breathing.

Beach remembers hearing the mother's cries as he walked to the front door. In one of the bedrooms, a baby girl was lying on a bed, surrounded by medical equipment.

The baby suffered from the birth defect spina bifida and had undergone a tracheotomy, a surgery that makes an opening in the windpipe to better allow air into the lungs. Beach tried CPR.

His eyes close as he tells the story.

I Did What I Had to Do

"I couldn't get breaths into her, and her heart had stopped," Beach says. "I just did what I thought I had to do."

He moved the child to the kitchen table to stabilize her. Then he covered her mouth and nose, while sucking mucus and blood from the opening in the windpipe. Thinking the airway was clear, Beach spat the fluid on his sleeve and tried another round of CPR.

Members of the volunteer rescue squad showed up and took over. "I remember them saying she was gone, and it really hit me hard," Beach says. "It bothered me a long time. . . . What could I have done different?"

When Beach says this, he is not speaking of the equipment he could have worn or the shots he could have taken to prevent the other casualty that day.

Living with Hepatitis C

Beach has had no problem finding folks willing to sacrifice half their liver for him. It's finding the right person that has proved difficult.

With about 16,000 people nationwide, waiting for a liver transplant, Beach isn't banking on a deceased organ donor. He's looking for a living donor—someone willing to sacrifice a portion of his or her healthy liver, the only organ in the human body that regenerates.

He eases his body onto the sturdy green recliner, leans back, resting his head near a crocheted blanket that's draped over the chair. His ankles are swollen, his stomach

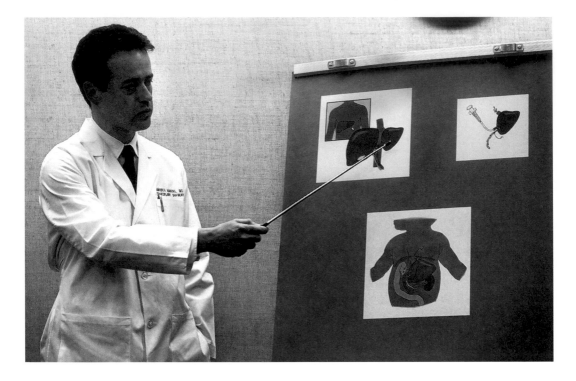

In March 1998 Dr. Amadeo Marcus of the Virginia Commonwealth University Medical Center speaks to the press about the second adult-to-adult liver transplant performed at the university's transplant center. Since then the center has performed 110 living donor surgeries. (AP Images)

as big as a basketball from water retention. His liver barely functions after 20 years of living with the hepatitis C he contracted the night he tried to save the little girl.

He stays off his feet most of the time. He has adopted a low-sodium diet and drinks homemade juices made from fresh fruits and vegetables every day between 11 A.M. and noon. Hot baths every morning and night soothe the cramping in his legs.

Most Sundays, Beach can't go to church because being around lots of people is exhausting. Worse, he could catch something that would further weaken his body. Occasionally, he walks to the end of his road or makes the drive to the grocery store with his wife, staying inside the car as she shops.

Beach is only 52. He wants to return to work as an investigative lieutenant with the Smithfield Police Department. He wants the strength to go back to Smithfield Assembly of God, the church where he volunteers as the sound man for worship services and other occasions. He wants the next 25 years with his wife, Kathie, to be just as good as the first quarter-century.

For more than a decade, Beach took trial drugs and tried other procedures. His body never responded to the experimental treatments. Still, he watched others with liver trouble die while he lived.

"God's hands have been on him all these years," Kathie Beach says, glancing at her husband.

In Search of a Living Donor

At Virginia Commonwealth University [VCU] Medical Center in Richmond, where Beach is being treated, about 140 patients need a new liver. Doctors at VCU's Hume-Lee Transplant Center performed the second adult-to-adult living-donor liver transplant in the nation in 1998, said April Ashworth, coordinator of the center's liver transplant and living-donor programs. Since then, they've done about 110 of the living-donor surgeries.

"It's really another option for a patient, and it decreases the waiting time," Ashworth said. Patients in search of a living liver donor must find someone who is healthy with a similar build, has a matching blood type, and meets other criteria. Ashworth screens potential donors over the phone for at least 30 to 45 minutes. Those who pass travel to Richmond for three to four days of medical testing.

Hume-Lee doesn't keep a list of people willing to be living liver donors. With each case, someone—usually a family member—must be willing to step up to the plate.

It's a lot to ask, Ashworth said, for an otherwise healthy person to volunteer for a 10- to 12-hour surgery. Odds are they'll make it out alive, but you never know. So the center takes a "conservative" approach when identifying donors, taking every step to rule out those with pre-existing medical problems. "We wouldn't even do this procedure if we had enough deceased donor organs," Ashworth said.

During the surgery, doctors remove 50 to 60 percent of the donor's liver, which will regenerate within two to four weeks. The recipient's old liver is then replaced with the donated organ. If things go as planned, the donor will be out of the hospital in five to six days. But work is out of the question for at least four weeks. Follow-up care, along with the initial evaluation and the surgery, are covered by the organ recipient's insurance.

> ## FAST FACT
>
> It takes about four weeks after exposure to hepatitis C to detect hepatitis C antibodies.

Ken Schuler knows the drill. He donated a liver in 1999—to a stranger, a 39-year-old woman whose story he heard about from the television news.

Schuler, who lives in Linville, Va., endured a liver biopsy, chest X-rays, a meeting with a psychiatrist and other screenings before learning he was a match. He had the surgery in April and was back to normal three months later, his recovery hampered only by an unrelated kidney stone that developed.

At the time, people called Schuler crazy. They asked, why would you risk your life for someone you've never met? "It was like seeing someone drowning," he said. "You don't worry about whether the water's cold."

Nothing's Been the Same

The words stung: "unfit for duty." The message, delivered by Beach's doctor in early fall, was no easy pill to swallow for a police lieutenant who's a former able-bodied seaman and Virginia Marine Police captain.

It started in May with a trip to the Sentara Obici Hospital emergency room. There were more hospital visits, many more. Beach learned his liver was in the advanced stages of cirrhosis. "My liver function was not anywhere close to where it should be," he said. "The rest of me was in good health: my heart, my lungs."

Nothing's been the same since. Beach tried to work at first but he tired quickly. Words, names, other details once ever-present in Beach's sharp mind began to escape him as his ammonia levels fluctuated. His wife—"the love of my life and my best friend," Beach says—has to handle the bills now.

So many friends and strangers, more than Beach could have imagined, have called to offer to be donors. Co-workers have said they'll donate their sick leave. Community members opened a bank account to help Beach pay for medical bills not covered by insurance.

If Beach finds a living-donor match, it's likely he'll be in the hospital about two weeks. But the doctors will monitor his progress for a lifetime. They'll give him anti-rejection medication so his body will accept the new liver. But it might be a fight.

And even if Beach's body wins that battle, it might not be able to keep the hepatitis C from destroying his new liver.

Beach reaches next to his recliner to retrieve his Bible. He wants to read aloud the third chapter of James, verse 13. It's a passage that's touched him during recent devotionals.

Beach peers through his rectangular-framed glasses, perched on a face that's gaunt and yellowed with jaundice. "Who is wise and understanding among you?" he reads. "Let him show it by his good life, by deeds done in the humility that comes from wisdom."

Life Is Difficult for Chinese Living with Hepatitis B

Tan Ee Lyn

In the following viewpoint Tan Ee Lyn describes the tragic plight of Chinese people who are carriers of the hepatitis B virus. According to Tan, more than 100 million Chinese people carry the virus, most of them contracting it when small children. Unlike other places around the world, where one's hepatitis B carrier status is primarily unknown and generally not considered frightening, in China hepatitis B carriers are feared and treated like outcasts. The author describes how Chinese hepatitis B carriers suffer prejudice and discrimination throughout their lives. Tan is an international journalist. She has written for Reuters, the *Mirror*, and the *International Herald Tribune*.

Madam Yan and 11 other mothers in China turned to the All-China Women's Federation for help after their toddlers were denied places in kindergarten after testing positive for the Hepatitis B virus.

"When I see other children going to school happily and mine is alone, my heart drips with blood," Yan wrote.

Hepatitis B is preventable through vaccination and there are drugs to control the replication of the virus in carriers, such as Yan's child, who shows no symptoms.

Fear of the Virus Causes Hysteria

Risk of infection through casual contact is minimal, and in many places worldwide, most carriers go about their own business whether in school or at work, facing little or no discrimination. But in China, fear of the virus has reached hysterical proportions, health experts say.

Ignorance and relentless advertisements by drug-makers making misleading claims about the disease and touting all kinds of magic cures have built a climate of terror surrounding the virus, and discrimination against carriers, they add.

Many schools, universities and companies now subject students and staff to regular health checks to screen for the virus.

Toddlers who test positive are refused entry to school, older students are expelled, men and women can't find work and some couples are forced into separation by terrified in-laws.

Qing Song, an activist who helps carriers fight discrimination at work, related a case where a young pregnant woman discovered her carrier status during a prenatal check. "Her mother-in-law advised her to abort the child and fix her own health before trying to conceive again. But after the abortion, she was forced into a divorce and driven out of the family home," said Qing, who is based in southern Shenzhen city.

Children Become Carriers for Life

Hepatitis B is endemic in parts of Asia and Africa.

Worldwide, there are 360 million carriers and a whopping third of that, or between 120–130 million, are in China. China's hepatitis B rate has historically been high but the reasons are unclear and it is not known if it may be due to genetic susceptibility.

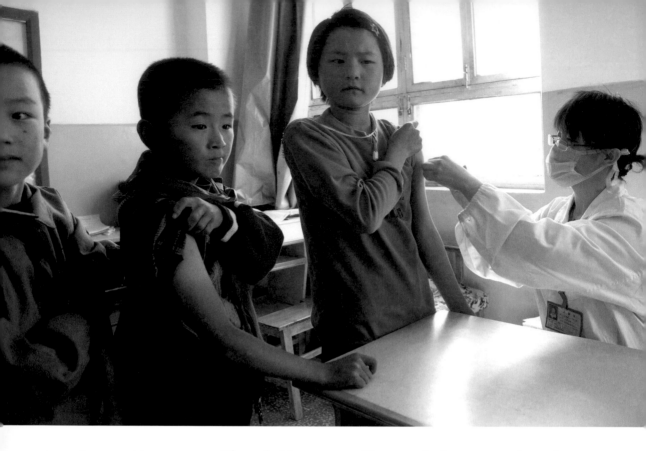

An estimated 120 million to 130 million Chinese are hepatitis B carriers, which prompted the Chinese government to begin free vaccination of children in 2002. (Aaron Deemer/ Bloomberg News/ Landov)

Though 10 percent of its population are carriers, that figure is believed to be as high as 17 percent in its southern provinces, such as Guangdong and Guangxi.

The chief mode of transmission is from mother to child. Others include sex, blood transfusions and contaminated needles, including the reuse of needles to vaccinate children, which was a common practice in China up until recently.

While a mature immune system in an older child or adult can flush out the virus, this is not the case for children under the age of 5 who contract the virus. It remains in their bodies, replicating quietly.

Drugs can only control the virus but not get rid of it and most of these younger children become carriers for life. One in four of them are at risk of developing cirrhosis—scarring of the liver—or liver cancer later in life.

The Chinese government introduced free universal vaccinations for newborns in 2002, but actual coverage is inconsistent. Medical experts say more babies are vaccinated in the cities than in rural areas.

Carriers of Disease Face Discrimination

The government has tried to stop discrimination in recent years, reversing an age-old policy banning carriers from the civil service. Last year [2007] it banned companies from screening employees for the virus in health checks and using a positive test result as a condition to fire staff or reject new hires.

But these laws are difficult to enforce. "Employers don't give a reason anymore. They say you are a danger to others or that you will suffer prejudice. They persuade you to resign and they don't have to compensate you," said a lawyer, who carries the virus and declined to be identified.

"It (carrier status) has deep repercussions whether in employment, marriage or social relationships. If people know you have it, they will reject you because they think you will infect them," said Ah Peng, who applied to work at a hotel but was rejected after a pre-employment health check showed he had the virus.

> **FAST FACT**
>
> According to the World Health Organization, hepatitis B carriers worldwide number around 350 million.

Tragic Consequences

Consequences of such discrimination can be tragic.

Walter Shual managed to escape health checks at his company for three years, but depression and the constant stress of being found out finally drove him to quit his job and leave China. "You can't imagine the situation if your colleagues come to know you're a carrier. People are selfish and ignorant because of misleading (information) from the government and some doctors," said Shual, who works at a scientific institute in South Africa.

Ah Tian, also a carrier, said his childhood friend died at the age 26 from an overdose of drugs that a doctor prescribed with an assurance that it would get rid of the virus.

"There is so much prejudice, suffering, pressure and people are desperate, he was so anxious to get well," said Ah Tian. "This virus affects my job, family and love life, what else can be closer to us? Even my brother wouldn't sit at the same table with me. I think of suicide sometimes."

GLOSSARY

acute Of abrupt onset, in reference to a disease. Acute often also connotes an illness that is of short duration, rapidly progressive, and in need of urgent care.

acute hepatitis The initial stage of viral hepatitis following infection.

alanine transaminase (ALT) A liver enzyme used as a marker for liver disease.

albumin A protein manufactured by the liver.

alcoholic hepatitis Inflammation of the liver caused by chronic ingestion of alcohol.

alcoholic liver diseases Diseases caused by excessive drinking that include fatty liver, or steatosis; liver inflammation, or hepatitis; and cirrhosis.

antibody A substance formed in the body in response to a foreign body, such as a virus, which can attack and destroy the invading foreign body or virus.

antiviral A drug used specifically for the treatment of viral infections.

aspartate transaminase (AST) A liver enzyme used as a marker for liver disease.

autoimmune hepatitis A disease in which the body's immune system attacks liver cells, causing inflammation of the liver.

bilirubin A potentially harmful by-product of the breakdown of old red blood cells that is normally excreted in bile. Elevated blood levels of bilirubin indicate liver disease. It is responsible for the yellow discoloration in jaundice.

carrier	A person who, after recovering from a viral infection, continues to carry the virus in the blood and can pass it on to others who may then develop infection.
chronic	Refers to diseases or habits that last a long time, recur, or are difficult to cure.
chronic hepatitis	Liver inflammation lasting longer than six months.
cirrhosis	A consequence of chronic liver disease characterized by replacement of liver tissue by fibrous scar tissue as well as regenerative nodules, leading to progressive loss of liver function. Cirrhosis is most commonly caused by alcoholism, hepatitis B and C, and fatty liver disease.
coinfection	Having two or more viral (or bacterial) diseases at the same time.
compensated cirrhosis	The liver is heavily scarred but can still perform many important bodily functions.
decompensated cirrhosis	The liver is extensively scarred and unable to function properly.
elevated liver enzymes	Higher than normal levels of the liver enzymes alanine transaminase (ALT) and aspartate transaminase (AST) in the blood that indicate inflamed or injured liver cells.
end-stage liver disease	The liver has completely broken down and is unable to perform its job.
fatty liver	Also called steatosis, a buildup of excess fat in liver cells.
fibrosis	An accumulation of tough, fibrous scar tissue.
hemoglobin	The protein in red blood cells that carries oxygen.
hepatic	Having to do with the liver. From the Latin *hepaticus* derived from the Greek *hepar* meaning the liver.
hepatitis	Inflammation of the liver from any cause.

hepatitis A	An inflammation of the liver caused by the hepatitis A virus (HAV), formerly referred to as infectious hepatitis.
hepatitis B	An inflammation of the liver caused by the hepatitis B virus (HBV), formerly referred to as serum hepatitis.
hepatitis C	An inflammation of the liver caused by the hepatitis C virus (HCV), previously known as non-A, non-B hepatitis.
hepatitis D	An inflammation of the liver caused by the hepatitis D virus (HDV).
hepatitis E	An inflammation of the liver caused by the hepatitis E virus (HEV).
hepatocellular carcinoma	A dangerous cancer of the liver that may develop in patients who have had hepatitis.
hepatocyte	A liver cell.
incubation period	The interval from initial exposure to an infectious agent, such as a virus, and the first symptoms of illness.
interferon	A small protein that helps the body protect itself from foreign invaders. Synthetic interferon is used as an antiviral medication to treat hepatitis.
jaundice	Yellowing of the skin (and whites of the eyes) when pigments such as bilirubin, normally eliminated by the liver, collect in high amounts in the blood.
liver	A vital organ present in vertebrates and some other animals. The liver has several important functions, such as protein synthesis; fat and carbohydrate metabolism; formation and secretion of bile to aid in the intestinal absorption of fats and the fat-soluble vitamins; elimination of harmful biochemical products produced by the body, such as bilirubin and ammonia; and detoxification of drugs, alcohol, and other environmental toxins.
liver biopsy	A procedure in which a small sample of the liver is removed to analyze for abnormal liver conditions.

liver transplant	Surgery to remove a diseased liver and replace it with a healthy liver (or part of one) from a donor.
living donor	A living person who donates an organ or part of an organ for transplantation into someone else.
morbidity	A disease condition or the occurrence or rate of a disease within a population.
mortality	The occurrence or rate of death within a population.
necrosis	Cell or tissue death.
pegylated interferon	Interferon with an attached polyethylene glycol (PEG) molecule. This form of interferon has a longer half-life in the body. Also called peginterferon or Peg-Intron.
pegylation	A process in which polyethylene glycol (PEG) molecules are attached to proteins in order to extend their activity in the body.
RNA virus	A virus that has RNA (ribonucleic acid) as its genetic material.
ribavirin	An antiviral medication approved for use in combination with interferon to treat chronic HCV infection.
steatosis	Buildup of excess fat in the liver, also called fatty liver.

CHRONOLOGY

B.C.   ca. 2000   First recorded references to jaundice; i.e., hepatitis, epidemics.

ca. 460–370   Jaundice (likely caused by hepatitis A) is described in the Hippocratic Corpus.

A.D.   ca. 751   Pope Zacharias recommends that "patients with jaundice be isolated lest others catch the contagion."

ca. 1600–1700   In *British Folk Medicine*, snails are recommended to treat jaundice.

1725   The term *hepatitis* is coined by J.B. Bianchi.

1819   French physician René Laennec, inventor of the stethoscope, gives cirrhosis its name, using the Greek word for "tawny," *kirrhos*, referring to the yellow nodules characteristic of the disease.

1883   The first recorded outbreak of serum hepatitis (hepatitis B) is provided by A. Lurman, who reports 191 cases of jaundice developing two to eight months after smallpox vaccination of dock workers in Germany.

1908   S. McDonald postulates that infectious jaundice is caused by a virus.

1914–1918   Large-scale epidemics of infectious jaundice (i.e., hepatitis A) occur during World War I.

1930	The first theory as to the pathogenesis of liver cirrhosis is advanced by German pathologist Robert Rossle.
1939–1945	Large-scale epidemics of infectious jaundice (i.e., hepatitis A) occur during World War II.
1943	The terms "infectious hepatitis" and "serum hepatitis" become common.
1947	F.O. MacCallum differentiates infectious hepatitis, which is spread by contaminated food and water, from serum hepatitis, which is spread by blood. He calls infectious hepatitis "hepatitis A" and serum hepatitis, "hepatitis B."
1963–1965	Baruch Blumberg and Harvey Alter discover the hepatitis B surface antigen (HBsAg). The antigen is referred to as the "Australian antigen" because it was first isolated from the blood of an Australian aborigine.
1967–1968	Baruch Blumberg, Kazuo Okochi, Alfred Prince, Alberto Vierrucci, and colleagues report that the Australian antigen is involved in the development of hepatitis B.
1969	Irving Millman and Baruch Blumberg receive a patent for using the Australian antigen to prepare a hepatitis B vaccine.
1970	D.S. Dane discovers whole hepatitis B virus particles in blood samples examined with the electron microscope.
1972	Laws are passed in the United States requiring testing of donor blood for HBsAg antigen.

1973–1974   Stephen Feinstone and colleagues and Maurice Hilleman and colleagues discover and describe the hepatitis A virus.

1977   Mario Rizzetto and John Gerin discover hepatitis D.

1980–1982   Maurice Hilleman and colleagues derive a hepatitis B vaccine from pooled blood. It is granted a license and approved for general use.

1983   Mikhail Balayan describes the hepatitis E virus.

1983–1986   William Rutter and colleagues derive a recombinant hepatitis B vaccine from yeast, which is approved for use. This vaccine is called the second generation hepatitis B vaccine.

1987   Scientists Michael Houghton, Qui-Lim Choo, and George Kuo clone and identify the hepatitis C virus as the cause of transfusion-related non-A, non-B hepatitis.

1990   Blood screening for hepatitis C begins.

1991   The U.S. Advisory Committee on Immunization Practices (ACIP) recommends hepatitis B vaccination for all infants in the United States.

1995–1996   Merck is granted the first general use license for the hepatitis A vaccine. SmithKline Beecham develops another hepatitis A vaccine.

2001   The Food and Drug Administration approves a stand-alone package of REBETOL (ribavirin) capsules, an antiviral drug for use with INTRON A (interferon alfa-2b) for the treatment of chronic hepatitis C infection.

ORGANIZATIONS TO CONTACT

The editors have compiled the following list of organizations concerned with the issues debated in this book. The descriptions are derived from materials provided by the organizations. All have publications or information available for interested readers. The list was compiled on the date of publication of the present volume; the information provided here may change. Be aware that many organizations take several weeks or longer to respond to inquiries, so allow as much time as possible.

American Association for the Study of Liver Diseases (AASLD)
1001 N. Fairfax St.
Ste. 400
Alexandria, VA 22314
(703) 299-9766
fax: (703) 299-9622
www.aasld.org

AASLD is an international organization of scientists and health care professionals committed to preventing and curing liver disease. The association sponsors several major conferences each year in clinical, basic, hepatitis, or pediatric hepatology. It publishes two monthly journals, *Hepatology* and *Liver Transplantation*, which provide the latest research findings for hepatology and surgery of the liver.

American Liver Foundation (ALF)
75 Maiden Ln.
Ste. 603
New York, NY 10038
(212) 668-1000
fax: (212) 483-8179
www.liverfoundation.org

ALF was founded in 1976 by the American Association for the Study of Liver Diseases. The foundation seeks to promote and provide education about liver diseases and liver health and support research for the prevention, treatment, and cure of liver disease. ALF advocates on behalf of millions of Americans living with liver disease. Its e-newsletter, *Liver Update*, provides up-to-date information about liver disease.

Division of Viral Hepatitis National Center for HIV/AIDS, Viral Hepatitis, STD, and TB Prevention (NCHHSTP) Centers for Disease Control and Prevention
1600 Clifton Rd.
Mailstop G-37
Atlanta, GA 30333
(404) 718-8500
fax: (404) 718-8588
www.cdc.gov/hepatitis

The NCHHSTP is part of the Centers for Disease Control and Prevention (CDC), an agency of the U.S. Department of Health and Human Services (HHS). The center maximizes public health and safety nationally and internationally through the elimination, prevention, and control of disease, disability, and death caused by HIV/AIDS, viral hepatitis, other sexually transmitted diseases, and tuberculosis. Within the NCHHSTP, the Division of Viral Hepatitis monitors and investigates hepatitis infections in the United States, provides health care provider education and training, and promotes public awareness to prevent the transmission of hepatitis C. The division issues written recommendations and guidelines for health care workers and issues various reports about hepatitis. Additionally, the division publishes several brochures for the public about living with and preventing hepatitis.

GAVI Alliance (formerly Global Alliance for Vaccines and Immunization)
1776 I St. NW
Ste. 600
Washington, DC 20006
(202) 478-1050
fax: (202) 478-1060
www.gavialliance.org

The GAVI Alliance is an alliance of public and private organizations, such as the World Health Organization and the Bill & Melinda Gates Foundation, that is dedicated to creating greater access to the benefits of immunization around the world. The alliance focuses its resources on making advanced vaccine products available in the world's poorest countries and strengthening delivery systems to ensure that their children derive full benefit. Its Web site provides facts and figures about immunization around the world, as well as many publications highlighting the organization's accomplishments toward increasing global childhood immunization.

Hepatitis C Support Project (HCSP)
PO Box 427037
San Francisco, CA 94142
www.hcvadvocate.org

The HCSP is a nonprofit organization founded in 1997 to address the lack of education, support, and services available at that time for the HCV population. The organization's mission is to provide unbiased information, support, and advocacy to all communities affected by HCV and HIV/HCV coinfection, including medical providers. The organization's publications include the bimonthly *Hepatitis Journal Review*, the monthly newsletter *HCV Advocate*, and various fact sheets and other educational publications.

Hepatitis Foundation International (HFI)
504 Blick Dr.
Silver Spring, MD 20904
(800) 891-0707
fax: (301) 622-4702
www.hepfi.org

HFI is dedicated to the worldwide eradication of viral hepatitis. The foundation's mission includes teaching the public and hepatitis patients how to prevent, diagnose, and treat viral hepatitis; preventing viral hepatitis by promoting liver wellness and healthful lifestyles; advocating for hepatitis patients; and supporting research into prevention, treatment, and cures for viral hepatitis. Its Web site provides education, training programs, and materials for the public, patients, health educators, and medical professionals.

Hepatitis Research Foundation
553 Salt Point Turnpike
Poughkeepsie, NY 12601
www.heprf.org

The Hepatitis Research Foundation is a nonprofit organization that works to raise funds to support research into the treatment of chronic hepatitis C and hepatitis B infections and the development of a vaccine for hepatitis C. The organization's Web site provides information about hepatitis B and C and provides up-to-date information on hepatitis research funded by the organization.

Hepatitis Support Association and *Liver Health Today*
PO Box 667399
Houston, TX 77266
(713) 808-9536
www.liverhealthtoday .org

The Hepatitis Support Association is a nonprofit organization created in 2002 specifically to take over the operation of a national magazine called *Hepatitis*. Subsequently, the magazine's name was changed from *Hepatitis* to *Liver Health Today*. The magazine *Liver Health Today* is dedicated to providing the latest information on every aspect of hepatitis B and C, from treatment options, side effect management and research to alternative medicine and government assistance. The magazine's Web site and sponsored conferences help the public gain a better understanding of liver disease.

Latino Organization for Liver Awareness (LOLA)
PO Box 842
Throggs Neck Station
Bronx, NY 10465
(718) 892-8697
fax: (718) 918-0527
www.lola-national.org

LOLA is a national bilingual, bicultural organization dedicated to raising awareness on liver disease. The organization provides and sponsors informational materials, prevention and education community outreach programs, treatment and referral services, and support groups. It publishes a quarterly newsletter, provides educational materials to prisoners with HCV, and sponsors HCV public education campaigns to the Latino community and other underserved populations who suffer from liver disease in the United States.

FOR FURTHER READING

Books

Ghassan K. Abou-Alfa, *100 Questions & Answers About Liver Cancer*. Sudbury, MA: Jones and Bartlett, 2005.

James L. Achord, *Understanding Hepatitis*. Jackson: University Press of Mississippi, 2002.

Baruch S. Blumberg, *Hepatitis B: The Hunt for a Killer Virus*. Princeton, NJ: Princeton University Press, 2002.

Madeline Drexler, *Secret Agents: The Menace of Emerging Infections*. Washington, DC: Joseph Henry, 2002.

Lyle W. Horn, *Hepatitis*. Philadelphia: Chelsea House, 2005.

Kurt Link, *The Vaccine Controversy: The History, Use, and Safety of Vaccinations*. Westport, CT: Praeger, 2005.

Melissa Palmer, *Dr. Melissa Palmer's Guide to Hepatitis & Liver Disease*. New York: Avery, 2004.

Nina L. Paul, *Living with Hepatitis C for Dummies*. Hoboken, NJ: John Wiley & Sons, 2005.

Howard J. Worman, *The Liver Disorders and Hepatitis Sourcebook*. New York: McGraw-Hill, 2006.

Periodicals

John Carey, "Waging War on Hepatitis C," *Business Week*, February 21, 2006.

Laura Elder, "Lab Could Experiment on Non-Human Primates," *Galveston (TX) Daily News*, October 16, 2005.

Harvard Reviews of Health News, "New Drug May Aid Hepatitis C Treatment," April 30, 2009.

Marcy Holloway and Kristin D'Acunto, "An Update on the ABCs of Viral Hepatitis," *Clinical Advisor*, June 2006.

Internal Medicine Alert, "Should We Be Screening for Hepatitis C?" May 15, 2008.

Jet, "Natalie Cole: Staying Strong with 'Still Unforgettable' Music," December 8, 2008.

Christine Kilgore, "NIH Consensus Statement Surveys Hepatitis B Care," *Internal Medicine News*, December 1, 2008.

Sonya MacParland et al. "Hepatitis C Virus Persisting at Low Levels After Clinically Apparent Sustained Virological Response to Antiviral Therapy Retains Its Infectivity in Vitro," *Hepatology*, May 2009.

Amy Maxmen, "Slow and Down: To Fight an Infection or Illness, the Body Shifts into a Slow-Down Mode That Mirrors Some Symptoms of Depression," *Science News*, July 19, 2008.

Andrew Pollack, "HIV Lessons Used in Hepatitis C Treatment," *New York Times*, March 11, 2003.

Andy Stone, "Cyborg Therapy (Artificial Liver Machine)," *Forbes*, February 16, 2009.

Miriam Tucker, "Most Should Get Birth Dose Against Hepatitis B," *Family Practice News*, August 1, 2005.

Tor Valenza, "Stretching Limits of MRI," *Medical Imaging*, June 2008.

INDEX